High on Adventure

For Herrings

Stories of of Good, Clean, Spine-tingling Fun

by Stephen Arrington

Huntington House Publishers

Huntington House Publishers
P.O. Box 53788
Lafayette, Louisiana 70505

Library of Congress Card Catalog Number
94-74568
ISBN 1-56384-082-0

Printed in the U.S.A.

Story illustrations by *Julie Pace* of
Carol Chislovsky Design, Inc.

Book artwork and design by *Jaynell Trosclair*

Cover design and layout by *Melissa Savoie*

In loving memory of my big brother,
James Richard Arrington
(27 October 1945–21 May 1994)
who was my protector when we were young,
my role model as we grew older,
and is now my inspiration for helping others.

And so we know and rely on the love
God has for us. God is love.
Whoever lives in love lives in God,
and God in him.

—1 John 4:16

The greatest achievement was at first and for a time a
dream. The oak sleeps in the acorn; the bird waits in the
egg; and in the highest vision of the soul a waking angel
stirs. Dreams are the seedlings of reality.

—James Allen

Contents

Introduction

For God did not give us a spirit of timidity, but a spirit of power, of love and of self-discipline.

—2 Timothy 1:7

Childhood and teen-age dreams are the future foundations for adult realities. Unfortunately, during the confusion of growing up, many young people lose track of this important fact. We forget the magnificence and wonder of life as seen through a child's eyes. Anxiously hurdling towards adulthood, we suppress youthful fantasies in favor of more secure and stable goals. Many students wander through their school years without focus or direction. Later, the vibrancy of their young lives slowly dulls as they trudge into careers they do not enjoy and endure relationships that bring them little happiness. Finally, one day they wonder in utter confusion, "What happened to my dreams?"

The answer is, we let them fade away by choice. Surprisingly, this is a conscious decision; we literally decide to limit our goals and aspirations. The reasoning behind this foolishness is absurd. People voluntarily abandon their dreams in favor of self-imposed restraints. To say, "I can't do that," is to argue for our limitations. It is an unbeatable statement that destroys what are otherwise achievable goals.

The human mind and body are capable of astounding feats. Considering that the body is a servant of the mind brings this equation of life to one basic truth. Whatever the mind dares, the body can do (within actual physical limitations). A person who loses the use of their legs will probably not run the mile in under four minutes. Then again, the average wheelchair racer usually crosses a marathon finish line far ahead of most long-distance runners.

High on Adventure is about living life to its fullest, achieving goals, and discovering that dreams do come true. We should reach beyond our horizons with enthusiasm and view obstacles as challenges on which to sharpen our skills and ambitions. Each of our accomplishments breeds new dreams that become launching pads for future quests. Human potential always exceeds mere physical boundaries.

This book is also about pursuing happiness. Happiness is a state of contentment that washes away problems, nourishes our health, and brightens our disposition. Happiness is so important that the Constitution of the United States guarantees us the right to pursue it. Yet, for many of us, happiness is only a hesitant achievement and becomes seemingly less attainable as we grow older. Why?

The answer is that happiness, like dreams, comes from within—it is self-generated. We consciously choose, or allow ourselves, to be happy. Little children do not realize that happiness is a choice, they tend to be naturally happy simply because it is more fun. For them life is an adventurous game that is constantly full of new discoveries. As we grow older, our happiness becomes more dependent upon our perception of how we approach life.

I do not believe in age. Age is relative to one's appetite for life, a curiosity about everything

> around. It's the way you look at things, as though you were looking at them always for the first time. (Martha Graham)

The final factor in our perception of happiness deals with our attitudes about ourselves. The goal of *High on Adventure* is to reflect the wonder and great happiness found in a close and personal relationship with Jesus Christ. I will show why young Christians have boundless opportunities for adventure and for realizing childhood and teen-age dreams.

> If you remain in me and my words remain in you, ask whatever you wish, and it will be given you. (John 15:7)

High on Adventure is written to compliment my first book, *Journey into Darkness* (Huntington House Publishers, 1992), which is about choices. Good choices lift us up and bad choices pull us down. I also reintroduce some of my Cousteau friends, such as Jojo the dolphin and Amy the great white shark.

One

If one advances confidently in the direction of their dreams, and endeavors to lead a life which they have imagined, they will meet with a success unexpected in common hours.

—Henry David Thoreau

Standing at the stern of the Cousteau Windship *Alcyone*, I watch a 17½-foot-long great white shark silently glide by just beneath the shimmering water. A small tag beneath her dorsal fin identifies this shark as Amy. This is not good news. Amy has a particularly bad attitude, even for a great white shark. I decide to wait a few moments before jumping into the water. It is the only way for me to get down to my cage, which I can just barely see six feet beneath the surface. The cage is all but invisible.

Jean-Michel Cousteau is conducting an interesting experiment. He wants to see how a great white shark will react to an apparently cageless diver, that being me inside a hollow plastic tube. This extraordinary cage is the first of its kind. It is built entirely out of Lexan, a clear plastic that has been known to stop a 38-caliber bullet. Yet, standing at the back of the boat, I couldn't help wondering about the strength of this thin plastic. I mean, how does the impact of an ounce of lead traveling at several thousand feet per second compare to the massive concussion of a three-thou-

sand-pound shark doing thirty miles per hour? Watching the great white shark circling aggressively beneath my flippers, I have the distinct feeling that I am about to find out.

Usually diving down six feet to the cage is not that big a deal, but this morning Amy began showing abnormally high interest in my short journey. Is she devising a plan to catch me at the halfway point, I wonder?

Many people do not give great white sharks much credit for being very smart, then again most people have not gotten to know a great white up close and personal. Amy and I are getting to know each other a bit too well for my liking. She is what we refer to as a resident shark. Her home is Dangerous Reef, an appropriately named location for Jean-Michel Cousteau to conduct his little experiment.

Seeing a shark's dorsal fin knifing through the smooth water fifty yards from the boat, I decide to make a quick jump for the cage. Just as my flippers clear the stern, our cook abruptly shouts, "Shark!" Looking straight down, I suddenly see a dark gray form slipping out from under *Alcyone*.

In mid-air I realize that the shark in the distance is not Amy. The crafty predator has been hiding under the Windship's stern, and we are now on a collision course. An instinctive fluttering of my flippers and arms does not prevent me from splashing into the chilly water a moment later.

Instantly, my mask floods with water. A froth of bubbles from my panicked entry further obscures my vision. Yet, none of this prevents me from seeing the fast approaching shark. Amy is only six feet away, and she is smiling. It is a full-toothed, two-foot wide kind of smile that only a really big shark can effect.

During a life-threatening situation, it is amazing
how time slows down and what amazing thoughts run
through your mind. At the moment, I'm remember-
ing Jean-Michel Cousteau's witty comment at the dinner table last night, "If a shark is about to get you,"
he said with a laugh, "just punch it in the nose."

The shark rapidly filling my face plate happens to
weigh around three thousand pounds. No way was I
going to try punching out a great white shark. I instead did the only logical thing I could do—I ran.

Turning my back on a torpedoing great white shark
is a very scary decision, but my only chance for survival lay in a fast dash for the dubious safety of the
plastic cage. From the surface, the crew watches anxiously as I race away from Amy's massive chompers.
I swim so fast it astounds the crew, who would later
affectionately nickname me propeller-butt.

Meanwhile, underwater I frantically open the top
hatch of the cage and quickly pull myself inside an
instant ahead of the torpedoing shark. Through the
clear Lexan, I see Amy charging by, her pectoral fin
hits the cylinder, setting it to swinging in the wake of
her violent passage. She turns, furious at missing her
opportunity, and slams into the thin plastic. In anger,
she gnashes her teeth against the cage's thin walls.
From the inside, I peer into her gaping maw from
only inches away. It is an awesome sight; with sunlight
radiating through her gill slits, I can see several feet
down her cavernous throat. Surprisingly, there is a
shrimp clinging upside down to the roof of her mouth.
What is this I think to myself, "shark dental floss?"

Amy thumps the cage with her snout, then glares
at me, which is very intimidating considering that we
are eyeball to dark orb. I rap my knuckles against the
nearly invisible plastic just to reassure my subcon-
scious that there is actually a barrier there. Being

right up against each other, her huge size is astounding. She is over seven feet wide (from pectoral fin to pectoral fin). Her gaping mouth has numerous rows of thumb-size teeth. I couldn't help noticing how her upper jaw dislocates outward each time the teeth crash against the plastic cage. Watching the shark's free-floating dental work reminds me of a trick my grandmother pulled on me. The thought takes me back in time to when I was twelve years old.

It was winter in Southern California, my grandmother and I were watching the "Underwater World of Jacques Cousteau"; it was a documentary on sharks. I was on the floor wearing a swimsuit with flippers on my feet. As the divers descended into the water, I put on a dive mask and tried to hold my breath with them. Sitting there with my mask fogging up was pretty exciting stuff. Then, abruptly, my grandmother's face filled the dive plate, she had her false teeth half-out and was chomping loudly like a shark.

Our shouts of laughter lured my mother from the kitchen, "What are you two doing?" she asked.

"Mom," I answered happily, "when I grow up I'm going to be a diver for Jacques Cousteau."

"Stephen," she said, "you should only wish for dreams that can come true. Jacques Cousteau isn't going to hire some American kid who doesn't even speak French."

Luckily, I held onto my dream and went on to become a Navy frogman. That act laid the foundation for a future that would eventually lead to my becoming a chief diver for The Cousteau Society—and amazingly, I still do not speak French.

Thinking about Mom and Grandma, I imagine how fun it would be if they could see me inside this plastic cage with the great white shark chewing on it. Suddenly, I realize that Amy is not in sight. Looking frantically about, I cannot believe that I have lost track of a 17½-foot-long shark—that is until I glance downward.

Amy is torpedoing directly at the bottom of the cage—its weakest point. Only a thin row of hollow plastic tubes lay between the shark and her desire for a human banquet. I feel the hair standing out on the back of my neck, which, underwater, is a very unusual sensation. The shark slams into the plastic tubes driving the cage upwards a full two feet. Swimming vigorously at the top of the cylinder, I see the hollow tubes bulging as the shark forces its massive head between them. She bites the center tube chewing on it industriously, then begins shaking the cage violently. Just when I think she is going to eat her way inside, a lead ballast weight slides across the cage floor slamming into Amy's snout. She instantly retreats downward into the gloom.

Looking toward the surface, I see Jean-Michel and the cinematographer signaling from a steel cage hanging off to my left. By their cheerful handmotions, I know they successfully caught the event on film. Later, this and other footage would prove two things.

First, that sharks are unpredictable. Usually, they prefer to ignore humans in favor of chasing fish. During the seven month period I spent hanging beneath *Alcyone's* stern, we encountered sixty-four sharks, and only three of them actually made attack runs on my cylinder.

The second proof is of a more personal nature. Childhood dreams do come true, but we must help to unlock their doors. The key is to strive for discipline in all aspects of our lives, to try to do good works for others, and to focus our attention on God. When He opens a door for us, we must not hesitate to step through it.

Delight yourself in the Lord and he will give you the desires of your heart. Commit your way to the Lord; trust in Him and He will do this. (Ps. 37:4)

Two

If you believe, you will receive whatever you ask for in prayer.

—Matthew 21:22

My journey toward becoming a chief diver for The Cousteau Society actually began in an old hard-hat diving suit. This is the type of heavy gear that divers wore from before the turn of the century through World War II. It is a relic from another era, a time when divers used to stomp around on the ocean floor. The antique diving rig is laying on the stern deck of a worn-out tug boat in Los Angeles Harbor. Standing before me is a seasoned diving veteran wearing a sock cap and frayed sweat shirt. Willie is old enough to be my grandfather's father. He fits right in with the dilapidated tug boat and antiquated suit.

The U.S. Navy sent me here for what they call an orientation dive. I have applied for diving school. It is the late 1960s, and before the Navy is willing to waste any time or money training a rookie diver, they want to see how the recruit takes to being underwater.

I am sitting on a diving stool wearing a pair of Willie's threadbare long underwear to insulate me from the cold water. The shabby wool material itches and there are a few suspicious stains, but Willie has assured me that these are his lucky long underwear.

Apparently, all the recruits who wore these shabby drawers made it through diving school. Scratching my chest, I nervously watch him greasing the leather seals on the old helmet.

"So you want to be a diver, huh boy?" Willie has a beard full of gray stubble, skin that looks like creased leather and a chipped gold front tooth.

"Yes sir," I answer, eyeing the debilitated diving suit warily.

"Handsome peace of gear, ain't it?" Willie lays a prideful hand on the old dented helmet.

"Isn't that face plate cracked?" I ask. There is a crack running in three directions across the glass port.

"Ain't no big deal," Willie shrugs. "Suit's got a few holes in it too, but you won't be down that long."

"Holes, what kind of holes?" I'm not finding this reassuring at all.

"Look," Willie appears to be getting upset, "don't worry about what don't concern you. If too much water gets in your suit, I'll just pull you up."

"Ah, Willie," I know I'm asking too many questions, but can't stop myself, "just what constitutes too much water?"

"Let me know if the suit fills much above your waist," Willie is dragging over the frayed canvas and rubber suit in question, "otherwise you might be a bit too heavy for me to get off the bottom."

"That suit looks like a pair of old frayed sneakers." I know I shouldn't be complaining.

"It should," Willie's laugh has a sinister ring to it. "Converse, the people who manufacture high-top sneakers use to make these rubberized-canvas suits, too. Only they closed the plant about thirty years ago. This suit is practically one of a kind so don't be putting any new rips or tears in it."

I decide it might be better not to ask any more

questions. If Willie reports that I seem too nervous about the dive, it could kill my chances of getting into diving school, and I want to be a Navy frogman more than anything. I jam both feet into the canvas suit, which is soaking wet on the inside and smells rather strongly of mildew.

With the suit around my waist, Willie reaches over and grabs a tub of grease. "Here boy, stick your hands in here," he says with a reassuring grin.

"What?" I can't hide my shock, "That's grease."

"Course it's grease, I just put new wrist seals on the suit and don't want you ripping them with your paws," Willie is definitely upset.

I put both hands into the cold grease then shake off the excess. Willie doesn't notice that a glob of the grease lands in his beard, nor do I tell him.

"Now you just sit there and let old Willie dress you out," Willie is glaring, just daring me to say something. I silently watch him scratch his beard, unknowingly spreading the grease across his chin and onto his nose.

Lifting a brass breast plate, he places it around my neck, then bolts it to a rubber gasket on the suit. Next comes the brass and leather boots that weigh seventeen pounds a piece, followed by a seventy-five pound leather and lead belt. I am trying to adjust to all the weight when I see Willie beating on a valve with a hammer.

"What are you banging on?" the question just slips out accidentally.

"Your air valve is a mite stuck," Willie says, hitting it a final wallop. "That should do it." He picks up the helmet and plops it over my head before I can say anything. After locking it in place, he opens the face port with the spider-web cracks in the glass. "Now you just stand up, and I'll walk you over to the ladder. Be careful. The rig weighs one hundred and ninety-five pounds, so you might be a bit awkward."

As he closes the face plate, the helmet feels immediately confining, though it is kind of fun to look out through the port holes. I clomp over to the ladder, then begin climbing awkwardly down into the harbor.

"When the water reaches your helmet, grab a hold of the descent line and let go of the ladder," Willie is talking to me through the helmet's speaker. "Be sure to let yourself down slowly," he cautions. "You don't want to go and burst an ear drum on me."

As the water covers my helmet, I nervously reach for the rope and, saying a silent prayer, release my grip on the ladder. Instantly, I am plunging straight down. The grease on my hands keeps me from getting a grip on the rope. I slide rapidly downwards and slam into the bottom hard. The impact drives my heavy boots several feet into the harbor muck.

"Man, you sure must have been excited to get down," Willie's voice echoes through the helmet. "I got you at thirty-three feet already."

Abruptly, I can't believe that I'm really underwater. I start to take a step, then quickly realize that I am stuck in the thick harbor mud. It is also when I first notice the cold water seeping into my suit.

"Go ahead," says Willie, "walk around a bit."

It is very dark on the bottom of the harbor. There is almost no light penetrating the muddy water. Holding my hand up to the face plate, I can barely see my fingers as I wiggle them. Then, I realize that if I can see my hand, so can a shark. I quickly tuck both hands firmly out of sight under my armpits. And, that is exactly how I stay for the next fifteen minutes with cold water quietly creeping into my suit.

"You having fun down there, boy?" Willie sounds curious as to what I'm doing.

"Yeah, this is great." I know Willie will report my performance to the diver recruiting officer.

"So, you about ready to come up?" he asks.

The cold water inside my suit is already above my knees, so coming up is the best news I could have heard. "I guess so," I respond, trying to sound slightly reluctant to leave the sea bed.

The umbilical goes very taut, I have to work at freeing my boots, but they finally pull out of the soft mud with a loud squishy-sucking sound. Looking upwards through the murky water as I ascend, I see it is slowly getting lighter above me. For the last few fathoms, I briefly wonder what aquatic adventures the future holds; in any case, I hope it gets much better from here.

A goal is a dream waiting to be realized.

Three

Remember this: Whoever sows sparingly will also reap sparingly, and whoever sows generously will also reap generously.

—2 Corinthians 9:6

Diving school lasts the better part of a year. There are many types of Navy divers, and I have chosen to become a bomb disposal frogman. I like the idea that by disarming bombs, I can help prevent people from getting hurt. However, after joining an operational team, one of my earlier assignments is to save a shark—a really big shark.

Canton Atoll is in the Pacific Ocean well south of the Hawaiian Islands. It is an isolated island with a very large shark population. The people there are used to seeing all types of sharks, big reef and tiger sharks, cruising the outer reefs and sometimes slipping quietly into the lagoon.

Mini, however, didn't arrive quietly at all. She rode into the island's lagoon on the back of a typhoon. The storm-induced waves lifted her over a barrier reef trapping the massive shark inside the broad lagoon. This was of great concern to the people there because this is where they liked to swim, and suddenly they were stuck with a twenty-five-foot-long shark in their swimming pool. The U.S. Navy operated a base on the island, so everyone decided that this was a problem

for the Navy to solve—which is why I and my team of frogmen arrived on a fine summer day in late July.

Our mission is to blow a hole in the lagoon's barrier reef, so Mini can swim out. Everyone is anxious to save Mini because she is actually a friendly shark. Though whale sharks are huge (they are the world's largest fish), they do not attack people. They are docile filter feeders.

That afternoon we get our first look at Mini. She is cruising slowly just a few yards from our inflatable boat. I am perched on the rubber hull with my flippers hanging over the side and with a coil of rope in my hand. Attached to the rope is a small buoy. As the Zodiac maneuvers a little closer to Mini, my job is to jump into the water and attach the rope forward of her tail. The logic behind this idea is so we will know where she is when we blow the reef. If she is too close to the blast, the underwater pressure wave could hurt her.

Staring at the huge animal swimming just beyond my flippers, I am a little hesitant to get into the water with a fish twice as long as our boat whose last name happens to be shark. I know she is supposedly a harmless filter feeder, but her mouth is over five feet across, and there are numerous rows of teeth in there. I mean, if she is only a filter feeder, why does she need so many teeth? Anyway, the next moment, I roll into—or I may have been pushed into—the water. Instantly, the big shark swims over to check me out. I am holding my breath, and, of course, nothing happens. 'She really is a friendly shark,' I think happily to myself.

Mini is in the process of slowly swimming off when I remember the rope hanging in my hand. Kicking rapidly, I go after her and latch onto the whale shark's dorsal fin. For a minute or two, I just hang on, exhilarated that I am actually riding a shark. I rub her side like I would a horse, which turns out to be a mistake. Where people have hair follicles in their skin, sharks have small teeth, which are modified scales called denticles. Their skin is extremely tough and quite abrasive. I stare in awe at the tiny scratches in my hand. Later, I would learn that sharks sometimes rub against their prey to taste them before biting. Anyway, I now need to attach the rope, which turns out not to be easy. Imagine what it is like trying to tie a rope around a swimming shark that is the size of a small school bus. Somehow, I manage to do it without getting tangled up in the rope.

The next day, we blow a small hole in the reef. It is unfortunate that the blast kills some of the reef fish. So they are not wasted, we collect the fish and give them to the local people.

Now that Mini has a way out, the last thing we have to do is remove her line and buoy. Since I put the rope on, the other guys figure I should be the one to take it off, which is going to be challenging. Mini is in a bad mood. She does not like the rope and is swimming rapidly to try to shake it off. If she swims out through the hole in the reef we may not get another chance to remove the rope. So, we decide on a high speed approach.

The Zodiac comes in fast. I'm laying on the hull wearing a very sharp knife at my waist. As we pull alongside the rapidly swimming shark, I roll into the water and quickly swim for her dorsal fin and latch on. Taking several deep breaths, I realize I must time this perfectly. The rope has slipped further back towards the tail; a tail that is eight feet tall and sweeping rapidly from side to side. Taking a last deep breath, I let go of the dorsal fin and gliding back towards the threatening tail, I grab the rope and cut it in a single slash. For a moment, I feel the flush of success, then

I see the tail coming right at me. I have timed it perfectly wrong. An instant later, my face plate fills with the oncoming tail, then everything goes black. The impact is like a fastball hitting a giant catcher's mitt.

A few moments later, the guys are pulling me back into the Zodiac. "Wow, that's some bruise you got," offers one of the divers, "covers your whole face."

One of the guys takes a picture, "I got to show this to my kids, they'll never believe you were stupid enough—I mean willing—to cut the rope."

Several days later, we got a telephone call that Mini had left the lagoon and a word of thanks from the local people for all the fish.

Dreaming is the easy part; making dreams come true takes commitment and hard work.

Four

Wine is a mocker and beer a brawler; whoever is led astray by them is not wise.

—Proverbs 20:1

With my hand resting on the tiller of the small sailing boat, I look forward to the captivating adventure that waits just over the ocean horizon. A brisk morning breeze fills the sail as the little catamaran skims across the South Pacific lagoon. A flock of sea birds flies squawking in my wake, and further to the stern I see Kwajalien Atoll. I think of the other Navy frogmen who chose not to accompany me. I can still hear their laughing response, "We've been checking sunken wrecks for unexploded ordinance for three months. When we finally get a day off, why would we want to go dive on another one?"

"But this is the heavy battle cruiser *Prinz Eugen*," I reply. "During World War II, it was the only ship ever to sail with the German battleship *Bismarck*."

"So?" Comes the unenthusiastic reply.

"This will be an incredible dive," I urge. "The ship is completely intact with her full complement of nine massive twelve-inch guns."

"Let's go crack some beers," one responds.

"Yeah," echoes another. "I'm going to get rip roaring drunk!"

Casting off from the wooden pier, I watched my teammates saunter up the dirt path towards the harbor bar. As the wind caught the sail, I wondered that my friends chose to fog their brains with alcohol instead of going after a real-life adventure. The catamaran handled easily as I sailed out of the small marina.

A school of flying fish, abruptly leaping before the catamaran, disrupts the thoughts of my friends. I watch the unique fish gliding rapidly away and wish I had someone to share this adventure with. It is so beautiful in the solitude of the tropical lagoon. I gaze at cumulous clouds drifting across the horizon against a cobalt blue sky, then in the distance I see a lush green island. I head for its north shore where there is a white sand beach with tall coconut trees leaning over a pale blue sea. There, just a hundred yards offshore, sunlight glistens brightly on a huge brass propeller protruding out of the water. Lowering the sail, I arrive with high expectations at my destination.

Beneath the shimmering water, I see the massive ship laying on its side. The heavy battle cruiser was damaged during the Bikini Island nuclear tests. She sank on this reef with her stern barely protruding from the surf while the bow lies way below at a depth of 120 feet.

Quickly donning my diving equipment, I plunge into the cool, inviting water, then reach up and pull in an underwater scooter. For a moment I pause to stare at the wonder that awaits me. The water is clear and full of tropical fish. Below, I look at the massive dreadnought with its living canopy of colorful corals and waving sea fans. Triggering the scooter, I begin a spiraling descent into the cool water.

Riding behind an underwater scooter is like flying in slow motion. Pretending I am a World War II pilot, I do a wing over and go into a vertical dive. I fly over a twelve-inch gun turret that has fallen to the side of the wreck, then angle closer to the ship's wooden decks. Except for the colorful corals, there is little damage or rust on the superstructure. Multi-hued schools of fish, their scales glistening in the soft light, swarm the wreck, swimming into and out of the armored deck compartments. Continuing to play bomber pilot, I wind my way down closely paralleling the ship's superstructure. I can almost imagine the German gunners manning their stations to shoot me down.

The bridge looms ahead suddenly, where I see a small black-tipped reef shark cruising the open ports. Further below, the bow lies hidden in the foreboding darkness of deep water. Passing through a thermocline, a layer of cold water, it turns sharply colder. A chill runs down my spine. Diving alone can sometimes be a little scary—suddenly I have the feeling this is going to be one of those times. Warily, I glance over my shoulder; shockingly there is a huge fish right behind me. It is a giant grouper, easily over four hundred pounds. His bulging eyes glare coldly. Hoping he doesn't have a mean disposition, I aim the scooter right at him and charge forward. With several rapid beats of its huge tail the giant fish quickly disappears downward into the darkness below.

"Wouldn't you know it?" I think to myself, "just the direction I want to go in, too."

My depth gauge reads 104 feet; I am too close to turn back now. The gloomy water continues to get colder and darker, then finally I see the shadowed form of the bow. I have already determined to limit my bottom time, but, knowing that big predatory fish is somewhere out in the darkness, I promptly decide to retreat upwards to clearer and warmer water. Turning around, I keep imagining that big fish is lurking just over my shoulder.

Reaching the fifty-foot level without seeing a sign of old bug-eye, I begin to relax and decide to explore inside the sunken ship. Tying the scooter off to a hand rail, I cautiously swim into an open door just aft of the bridge. The glow of my dive light plays off pale soft sponges and causes a spider crab to run for cover; little clouds of silt trace his tiny steps across the deck. Going down a narrow corridor, I discover a rack of torpedoes and stop to investigate the captain's living quarters. Looking deeper inside the ship, everything is veiled in silt and darkness. My light doesn't satisfy me that nothing is hiding in the corners. Glancing at my air gauge, I decide to return to the scooter and continue my ascent.

Ten feet from the surface I pause for a two minute decompression stop. After attaching the scooter to a line hanging from the boat, I amuse myself by trying to make friends with a small fish. Unexpectedly, the fish flees in panic. Spinning around, I'm shocked to see old bug-eye is right behind me—lurking! I scream in surprise, which comes out as a blast of bubbles. Bug-eye jets for the bottom as I rocket for the surface and scramble up into the boat without removing my scuba tank or weight belt.

Quickly peering over the side, I see only empty water and feel the rapid beating of my heart.

A half hour later I am underway again, sailing into a light tropical rain. I enjoy the refreshing feeling of the rain drops and heel the catamaran tighter into the blustery trade winds. Entering the harbor, I see twin rainbows shimmering on the horizon. Quickly tying the small boat to the pier, I hurry off to find my friends. I can't wait to tell them about the giant grouper.

Entering the darkened bar, I am immediately assaulted by the heavy stench of cigarette smoke that hangs in a lingering cloud. Loud music blasts from the juke box, then I see my friends at the bar. One of them snores loudly, his head resting in a puddle of spilt beer. The others are completely drunk and arguing some foolish point. Fortunately, they don't see me as I quickly step back outside into the daylight.

Following a jungle path back towards the harbor, I smell the fragrance of tropical flowers and hear exotic birds singing from the lush foliage. Basking in the warm sunlight, I think how my friends have not only wasted an opportunity for adventure, they're ruining their minds and bodies. In an island paradise, surrounded with incredible adventure, they have chosen to deaden their brains in a darkened bar. Tonight, they will be surly and bad tempered; come morning, they will be sick and hungover.

It doesn't take a rocket scientist to realize that good choices lead to happiness and adventure, while bad choices breed corruption, sadness, and nightmares. The decision, as always, is ours to make.

> Who has woe? Who has sorrow? Who has strife? Who has complaints? Who has needless bruises? Who has bloodshot eyes? Those who linger over wine, who go to sample bowls of mixed wine. Do not gaze at wine when it is red, when it sparkles in the cup, when it goes down smoothly! In the end it bites like a snake and poisons like a viper. (Prov. 23:29-32)

Collecting my gear from the boat, I decide to make a night reef dive. In the dark of evening many strange and odd-looking marine creatures, not seen during the light of day, come creeping out of the reef's dark holes and crevices. Tonight will be an underwater Halloween adventure.

Five

Become the most positive and enthusiastic person you know.

—Jackson Brown

I arrive at the airport just after sunrise and immediately begin my pre-flight checks of the small airplane. It is overcast, as usual, on this cold winter morning. I am stationed at a naval air station near a small California coastal town. The ocean fog often sweeps in over the airport; by late morning it will burn off. But, I want to fly now, so I will need to get a special clearance to take off with the limited ceiling. I'm still in my flight training, and, though I don't yet have a pilot's license, I am allowed to fly solo. I have always wanted to learn to fly, so I saved enough money to make this dream come true.

Taxiing out onto the runway, I radio the tower and receive clearance for a limited-visibility take off. Pushing the throttle to maximum, the light plane rushes down the runway and lifts off into the morning light. I climb to three hundred feet then level off. The overcast is a solid blanket of fog fifty feet above the airplane. It is thrilling to fly at such a low altitude. I feel like I could reach out the window and almost touch the rapidly passing trees and telephone poles. Banking into a sharper turn than necessary, I point the plane toward a dry wash bed, and, using it as a guide, fly inland. Soon the fog blanket begins to dissipate, so I climb to five thousand feet to practice my maneuvers.

While still climbing, I pull the throttle back to idle. The plane slows and begins to shudder as it loses lift. This maneuver, known as a stall, is exactly what the plane does next. The right wing raises up as the small plane noses over and goes into a steep dive. Shoving the throttle to maximum and leveling the wings, I continue the dive allowing the plane to gain speed. At 110 MPH, I pull back on the wheel, kick in left rudder, and go into a tight banking turn. The gravity of the high-speed turn drives me deeper into the seat. I am so excited I could scream—so I do.

Two months later (June 1975), at the age of twenty-five, I would fulfill a childhood dream by earning my private pilot's certificate, which according to my instructor meant I am now the most dangerous object in the sky. He thought I tended to be a little too adventurous at the controls. Actually, flying an airplane is not an extraordinary feat. I certainly am not a special person, just a practical human being who does not believe in restricting his potential for adventure.

As I write this chapter, I think about a story in the newspaper (1 April 1994), laying on my desk. It is an article about someone who is very extraordinary. Rachel Carter is nine years old. Today, she became the youngest person to fly an airplane across the United States and back. This fourth-grader, who sits on a pillow so she can see out of the airplane's window, flew 5,506 miles in ten exciting days. Her father was along as copilot, but he kept his hands off the controls. Their trip began in San Diego, where the last words the crowd heard before the plane door closed were, "Dad, may I have the keys?"

The five-foot-tall, fifty-five pound pilot is quoted as saying, "I learned to follow your dreams if you ever have them. I mean, because a lot of kids, they have no dreams. But whoever does have a dream. I think they should follow it."

Most kids are not fortunate enough to have access to a plane which they can fly across the country. Yet, dreams should not idly wait for the right opportunity to come along either. If we want something bad enough, the first step is always to begin to pursue it. If we wait too long, the dream could fade into memory—which is a terrible fate for a dream that could have come true.

> *Delight yourself in the Lord and he will give you the desires of your heart. Commit your way to the Lord; trust in him and he will do this.* (Ps. 37:4)

Six

If a man does not keep pace with his companions perhaps it is because he hears a different drummer. Let him step to the music he hears, however measured or far away.
—Thoreau

I am again in a nose-down dive. Only this time, I am in the sky over the Hawaiian Islands, doing 140 MPH—without an airplane. The helicopter I jumped out of is a thousand feet above me as I hurl through the night sky. Beneath me, I see moonlight dancing on the rippling surface of the Pacific Ocean. At thirty-five hundred feet, I pull the rip cord and instantly feel the bite of nylon straps going snug as the parachute deploys above me. Then, all is quiet, but for the rustle of wind rushing through my canopy as I slowly drift across the star-filled sky.

Looking back down toward the water, I see the twin wakes of two black Zodiacs speeding in my direction. I activate a strobe light on my boot to aid their picking me up once I hit the dark water. This night-time parachuting operation is a standard part of our ongoing frogman training. Every three months, we are required to make a night jump into the ocean. Maintaining our jump qualifications is one of the more fun aspects of this exciting job.

Suddenly, I notice there is something not quite right with the pickup boats. I can tell that they are speeding in my direction, but they seem to be falling behind—which is very surprising considering these boats are extremely fast. Looking more closely at the ocean surface, I realize I'm not looking at moonlight dancing on the water as much as it is lunar light reflecting off the wind froth of white caps. Glancing back at the shoreline of Oahu, I realize there is a strong wind blowing, and it is hurling me straight out to sea.

For a heart-stopping moment, I consider the possibility of being lost in an empty ocean at night. The word *shark* even flutters through my thoughts an instant before my feet hit the water. A half-second later I am jerked back out of the water as my parachute, which is still full of wind, races straight out to sea. I am skimming across the surface, bouncing from white cap to white cap, face down. Salt water is shoveling up my nose at an appalling rate. I am in threat of drowning from nasal ingestion. Reaching desperately for a capewell, I trigger it, which releases one set of shroud lines. The wind spills from the parachute, and the canopy collapses, which is good until it falls over my head. Because it is not easy to breath under wet nylon, I desperately begin working my way toward the edge of the parachute. When I finally come up for a breath of air, one of the speeding Zodiacs narrowly misses running me over.

As the other frogmen pull me into the inflatable boat, I think next time I jump out of an airplane, I will ask the pilot to check the wind velocity first. By not paying attention to my environment, I could have made a fatal mistake. For a moment, I remember a high school friend who took a dare to jump off a cliff into a river swimming hole. The other kids incorrectly assumed he knew about the underwater rock that they naturally avoided. That one foolish mistake, a brief moment of inattention and bad judgement, has placed him in a wheelchair for life.

As the saying goes, "Look before you leap!"

Seven

Not only so, but we also rejoice in our sufferings, because we know that suffering produces perseverance; perseverance, character; and character, hope. And hope does not disappoint us, because God has poured out his love into our hearts by the Holy Spirit, whom he has given us.

—Romans 5:3–5

"You will never walk again," the doctor pronounces gravely. The patient at first refuses to believe this is happening. Then, slowly their already wounded spirit caves into itself in defeat. For the rest of their lives many handicapped people willingly accept their wheelchair sentences, not realizing that they have other possible options.

There are many ways to accomplish a goal, particularly if we have open, inquisitive minds and are willing to risk the unknown challenges that wait on the path to adventure. One such person is my friend Rusty.

Rusty arrives early at the dive boat. As usual, he is eager to get out to sea. His girlfriend helps wheel him aboard, while I shoulder his dive gear.

During most of the short voyage out to the Channel Islands, Rusty is at the bow watching for dolphins. At mid-morning we anchor in a sheltered bay. The rest of the divers are quickly in the water. It will take Rusty a bit longer to get ready, but he prefers it that

way. He carefully goes over his scuba equipment and won't accept any help getting ready. He says it is part of his discipline because he had to work very hard and even suffer some physical pain to become a scuba diver.

Several years earlier, Rusty was in a terrible automobile accident. He lost both legs, an eye, and most of one arm. The doctor said he would be confined to a wheelchair for the rest of his life. Rusty didn't believe it and was determined to prove otherwise.

After donning his tank, Rusty crabs awkwardly to the ladder, then tumbles over the side of the boat. I leap in an instant behind him. There is that initial shock as our wet suits fill with cold water, which our bodies quickly warm. Rusty looks over and grins. "Weightless again, I love it," he declares happily.

At the surface, we do a quick buddy check, then Rusty leads the way downward. He is surprisingly graceful considering he has only one swim fin attached to the stump of a leg. He wears a webbed glove on his one good arm to give him added propulsion and steerage.

Underwater a diver doesn't swim, he flies. Lacking gravity, Rusty and I soar through the upper branches of a giant kelp forest. Slowly, we weave our way downwards, swimming through a school of colorful fish, to the reef below. Rusty flips on a helmet light so he can peer into the reef's dark crevices, where he discovers a friendly moray eel. These shy creatures, despite a fearsome appearance, are relatively harmless. Opening a plastic bag full of dried dog food, Rusty begins to hand-feed the eel. Dozens of reef fish rush in to share, much to Rusty's delight.

As I look at my dive-buddy with all his finned friends, I wonder what the doctor would say if he could see him now. Maybe the next time he had to

say, "You will never walk again," he might hopefully
add, "but you could fly!"

It is not the strength of our bodies that counts,
rather it is the strength of our convictions.

> *But those who hope in the LORD will renew their
> strength. They will soar on wings like eagles; they
> will run and not grow weary, they will walk and not
> be faint.* (Isa. 40:31)

Author's note: For more information on scuba diving op-
portunities for wheelchair adventurers call or write the
Handicap Scuba Divers Association or consult the regional
NAUI or PADI director through your local dive shop.

Eight

Blessed is the man who finds wisdom, the man who gains understanding, for she is more profitable than silver and yields better returns than gold. She is more precious than rubies; nothing you desire can compare with her. Long life is in her right hand; in her left hand are riches and honor. Her ways are pleasant ways, and all her paths are peace.

—Proverbs 3:13–17

Standing at the plunging bow of the *Alcyone*, I listen to the whispery sound of water rushing past the windship's hull as she races into the warm tropical night. Above me, the heavens are radiant. At sea, there are no city lights to dim the nighttime majesty of the stars and planets. A couple of points off the bow, I stare in awe at the Southern Cross. The shield-like configuration of the stars rides low on the horizon like a beacon pointing the way to unknown adventures.

When I was a kid growing up in Southern California, on summer nights I often camped in my own backyard. Under the mysterious glow of a flashlight's beam, I enjoyed reading adventure stories, mostly about sailors of the past and their tall sailing ships. My heroes were real life explorers discovering the wonders of distant oceans and far off lands. Then, turning off my flashlight and staring into the night sky, I would look for the Big Dipper and pretend it was the Southern Cross. In the theater of my mind, I became one of those adventurous explorers.

Now, as I feel the powerful hum of *Alcyone's* engines vibrating up through the soles of my sneakers, I ponder the wonder of dreams that actually come true. For a moment, I think about that little boy growing up in a California suburb. Though much older now, that youth is still very much a part of me. I chuckle out loud as I realize that in my jeans, T-shirt and high-top Converse sneakers, I still dress like him. There is even a flashlight in my hand and on the windship's deck lays my old flannel sleeping bag. I couldn't resist bringing it along when Jean-Michel Cousteau asked me to join his team of divers. Under the bright beam of the flashlight, I can still read the faded Coleman label where my mother stenciled my name to keep me from losing it at YMCA camp. After my watch, I am planning on sleeping out under the stars just like when I was a kid. Turning off the flashlight, I return to the bridge.

Sitting down in the captain's chair, I first check the radar screen. Its soft green glow paints a mostly clear horizon. There are no other boats within its twenty-mile range. Since we are crossing deep water in an open ocean, this will be a relaxing watch. I do a quick sweep of the various gauges to make sure all is well with the engines and check the compass to ensure the windship is on course. Secure that all is well, I open my Bible to the Book of Proverbs and begin to read.

> The proverbs of Solomon son of David, king of Israel: for attaining wisdom and discipline; for understanding words of insight; for acquiring a disciplined and prudent life, doing what is right and just and fair; for giving prudence to the

simple, knowledge and discretion to the young—
let the wise listen and add to their learning,
and let the discerning get guidance. (Prov. 1:15)

"Wow," I think to myself, "can there ever be an
introduction to a book more powerful than that?"
King Solomon, a man who had all that a kingdom
could provide, a king of great knowledge, with vast
wealth and an incredible diversity of worldly experi-
ences; a man who knew and was blessed by God; from
the distant past his words, inspired by the Lord, span
time to reach out and touch us with wisdom and with
guidance. What a wonder this is.

I close the Bible, but do not set it down as I think
about what I just read. All of us want to live happy,
satisfying lives, and that one simple paragraph tells us
exactly how to make this happen.

A gentle chiming from the ship's chronometer
announces the top of the hour. It is two o'clock in the
morning and time for me to plot our location. At the
chart table, I draw intersecting lines on an Indian
Ocean map. We are exactly three hundred miles south-
east of Indonesia and a quarter of a mile off course.
At the helm, I turn a small black knob two clicks to
port. The autopilot instantly responds as *Alcyone* turns
slightly into the wind.

For a moment, I think how the Bible is very much
like my map and autopilot. As we plot our life's jour-
neys, we sometimes get a little off course. The winds
of the world often try to blow us in wrong directions
or into troubled waters. Yet, by regularly reading the
Bible, we can more easily find our way back to the
right path; the path that leads to happiness, self satisfaction, and a closer relationship with our Creator.

Opening the Bible again, I return to a proverb
that greatly influenced me as a child and is now an
adult foundation for my life's quest.

Buy the truth and do not sell it; get wisdom,
discipline and understanding. (Prov. 23:23)

When I was a youth, growing up in a crowded Los
Angeles suburb, I knew that with discipline and focus,
I could realize my dreams. One day, I would see the
Southern Cross for real. Proverbs 23:23 was to be the
passport for getting me there. Now, the Book of Prov-
erbs is my guide for appreciating all that life offers.

Sitting at the helm of the windship, I again check
the radar, then quietly continue to read the Bible and
think about a man named King Solomon.

*I will study and prepare myself and then someday
my chance will come.* (Abraham Lincoln)

Nine

It is not what happens to you, but your attitude toward the happening that determines your happiness.

—Unknown

The Zodiac races across the choppy water, while I cling desperately to its wildly bouncing rubber hull. Jean-Michel Cousteau is at the throttle, and he is a man in a hurry. A large pod of humpback whales is moving rapidly through the water several hundred yards off to our port side. Jean-Michel wants to get well ahead of them so we can be waiting in their path and ready to film when they go by. The Zodiac rockets off a cresting swell, for a heart-thumping moment I am airborne, then the inflatable slams back into the water. I see the black rubber hull rushing up to meet my face; the impact nearly throws me into the water.

"Get ready," shouts Jean-Michel.

I glance over at our cinematographer, Michel DeLoire, who is eagerly watching the approaching whales. I too can't wait to get in the water. I have never swam with whales before and am bubbling with enthusiasm as I clutch my Nikonos underwater camera to my chest.

"Now," shouts Jean-Michel, as he cuts the engine.

Michel DeLoire grabs the big cinema camera, and we quickly roll out of the boat. Hitting the water, I begin kicking as fast as possible and am completely

surprised to see the Zodiac drifting slowly ahead of me. "Why am I not going anywhere?" I wonder, then am abruptly aware of what is wrong.

"Where are your fins?" shouts Jean-Michel.

Floating helplessly in the water, I am completely embarrassed. In the excitement of the pursuit, I have forgotten to put on my swim fins.

Jean-Michel quickly grabs them from the floor boards of the Zodiac and holds them just beyond my reach. "How is it possible, that my new chief diver could forget his little flippers?" Jean-Michel is greatly enjoying this moment.

With a snorkel jammed in my mouth there is little I can say, not that anything suitable comes to mind. So instead, I lunge for the fins and quickly begin strapping them on.

"You better hurry," laughs Jean-Michel, "I don't think the whales are going to wait for you."

Taking a deep breath, I dive quickly beneath the water. Below, I see Michel DeLoire swimming upward, but there is no sign of the whales. He grins at me as he holds up one thumb victoriously. He is obviously ecstatic. We surface together at the side of the Zodiac.

"Incredible," Michel DeLoire beams to Jean-Michel hoisting himself into the inflatable boat. There are a dozen of them, mostly big bulls.

"Any calves?" Jean-Michel asks hopefully.

"Yes," Michel DeLoire answers in his rich French accent, "a very little one, just a baby, maybe two- or three-weeks-old."

As I pull myself despondently into the Zodiac, Michel DeLoire looks curiously in my direction. "Where were you?" he asks, "the whales let me get quite close to them."

"My new chief diver forgot his flippers," Jean-Michel Cousteau answers flatly.

"Really," Michel DeLoire is grinning hugely, "you forgot your fins? But, how is that possible? You are a chief diver."

"Do you think we should tell Cindy?" asks Jean-Michel picking up the walkie-talkie.

"But of course." Michel DeLoire is enjoying himself immensely.

"You're not really going to tell Cindy?" I can't believe this is happening. Cindy, my wife-to-be, is skippering our support boat. I can see it several miles in the distance over toward the island of Maui. Further off, I see a host of other boats and know that most of them are probably monitoring our radio transmissions.

"Cindy, this is the Zodiac calling," Jean-Michel smiles at me.

"Cindy here," comes the prompt reply.

"I thought you would like to know that Steve was so excited to swim with the whales, he forgot to put on his fins."

"Really?" I distinctly hear Cindy giggling and a loud chuckle from one of the crew members in the background. "How embarrassing," Cindy sounds delighted.

"You should have seen him, his finless-feet were fluttering at warp speed, but he was slower than a drifting rubber boat."

I think Jean-Michel is trying to be entertaining for the rest of the listening audience on the other boats.

Abruptly, Michel DeLoire points and shouts, "The whales, they're coming back."

We quickly redon our masks *and* fins, then grabbing the cameras, Michel DeLoire and I throw ourselves back into the water. Taking several quick breaths, we dive rapidly downwards.

At first, all I see is empty blue water. Then, less than a hundred yards away I see the whales coming.

A large cow is leading the pod. She is fully forty-five feet long and weighs over a thousand pounds per foot. The other whales range around her. It is like watching a fleet of approaching eighteen-wheeler trucks. The humpback whales are absolutely huge and majestically beautiful. Swimming at the cow's side is the baby calf. Though only several weeks old, already she is the size of a mini-van.

At a depth of fifty feet, I level off and eagerly begin taking pictures. I am directly in the path of the approaching whales. I keep expecting the calf to shy away; instead she angles closer and passes just six feet from me. For a few seconds, I am able to swim at her side. Like most newborn baby animals she has large innocent eyes. As she passes, she does a double playful kick with her tail. "Is this an invitation to play?" I wonder. Swimming as fast as possible, I try to keep pace but fall rapidly behind. I am beside myself with excitement, yet need to return to the surface for a breath of air.

Beginning to swim upward, I see two large bull whales slightly above me and headed in my direction. If they stay on their course, I will have to wait for them to pass. As if sensing my need for air, the whales begin to turn to the right. Though they are still passing above me, I can continue my ascent by angling to their left. I watch a huge whale pectoral fin glide past just feet away, then the massive tail sweeps by. I can feel the force of the whale's underwater wake just before I break the surface gasping for air.

Back on the Zodiac, I tell Jean-Michel how the whales actually seemed to move to allow me a straighter shot to the surface.

"I assure you that was no accident," Jean-Michel answers knowingly. "Humpback whales almost always move to make way for a person in the water. I have even seen them purposely lift their pectoral fins out of the way to keep them from accidentally striking a diver who gets too close. In general, I think whales make better decisions about humans beings than humans are making about whales."

Considering the immense size of the two bull whales I just encountered, it is amazing to think that those two magnificent creatures purposefully changed their course to make life a little easier on a tiny creature like me. Going back through the corridors of my memory, I remember another time I got in the way of something much bigger than me—only that encounter ended much differently.

It was my first day at high school, and, like a lot of other freshmen, I was frantically trying to find one of my classrooms. I was rushing along a narrow sidewalk, arms loaded with books, when a tall senior stepped purposefully into my way. By the size of the chest I ran into, he must have been a lineman for the varsity football team. An instant later, I and my books were airborne and headed for a hard landing in a thick hedge. The senior thought it was quite amusing and even laughed, but that didn't stop him from threatening to bust my head open for not watching where I was going. Our encounter, though damaging to my pride, wasn't really that big of a deal. Yet, it bothered me that the big lug was actually having a good time roughing up a kid half his size.

The human being is the only animal capable of finding any enjoyment in cruelty. Yet, making right decisions in life is not complicated. Good choices lift us up, and bad choices pull us down. The Bible defines it much more eloquently:

> The eye is the lamp of the body. If your eyes
> are good, your whole body will be full of light.
> But if your eyes are bad, your whole body will

be full of darkness. If then the light within you
is darkness, how great is that darkness! (Matt.
6:22–24)

The question of our happiness in life is dependent upon how we look at the world and how we view
ourselves in it. If we purposefully allow ourselves to
make mistakes, those poor choices can lead us down
a very dark path indeed. A series of small mistakes,
unless interrupted in time, always leads to a chain of
bigger mistakes. And, before one knows it, the chains
and the darkness become very real.

In the dark, men break into houses, but by day
they shut themselves in; they want nothing to
do with the light. For all of them, deep darkness is their morning; they make friends with
the terrors of darkness. (Job 24:16–17)

My thoughts are interrupted by Jean-Michel, "You
know, I've never seen a chief diver jump into the
water before without his fins."

"I must have looked pretty foolish," I answer with
a chuckle.

"Don't worry about it," Jean-Michel grins. "At least
it isn't as bad as when you forgot all of the dive masks
on our last expedition to Cocos Island."

Jean-Michel is referring to my very first expedition
with the Cousteau team. Like thousands of other divers,
I had recently offered my services to The Cousteau
Society, not daring to hope that anything would come
of it. Imagine my surprise when they not only called,
but brought me in as a chief diver.

Several months ago, I had been in charge of taking a team to Cocos Island, which is three hundred
miles from Costa Rica. We were halfway there aboard
an eighty-five-foot sailing schooner, when we realized
all of our dive masks had been left in a box at a Coast
Guard base. We had to sail back to Costa Rica to

retrieve eight lousy dive masks. As the chief diver, I naturally got full responsibility for the mistake—which is a point Jean-Michel cheerfully reminds me of on a regular basis.

One of the early lessons I learned in life is that we all will make mistakes. To err is a natural part of the learning process. Mistakes can, and should be, turned into building blocks from which we lay a strong foundation toward becoming better people. The point is to take a lesson from our mistakes and hopefully not repeat them.

Happiness is found in being content to be yourself.

Ten

America is too great for small dreams.
—Ronald Reagan

The wild dolphin spins and twists in a joyful dance before our underwater camera. Jojo loves being filmed, particularly since he can acoustically see the motors and gears of the movie camera turning inside its housing. His pectoral fins flapping in obvious delight, he opens his mouth in a broad dolphin grin and giggles, releasing a buoyant stream of bubbles that rise in an iridescent cascade towards the surface.

Jojo lives and plays in the pale turquoise waters of the Turks and Caicos Islands. No one knows where this solitary bottlenose dolphin came from, nor why he has such a strong affection for people. For reasons of his own, Jojo prefers human companionship over life in a dolphin pod. To find out more about this unique dolphin, Jean-Michel Cousteau brought our small flying team to investigate.

The Princess Alexandra Land and Sea Park is Jojo's home. The eastern border of the park is a long white sand beach with a sprawling Club Med resort. Jojo shares his domain with a multitude of people: swimmers, water and jet skiers, wind surfers, and scuba divers. One of his favorite activities is playing buoy bashing with the local kids. They sit on anchor buoys while Jojo charges and knocks the buoy out from

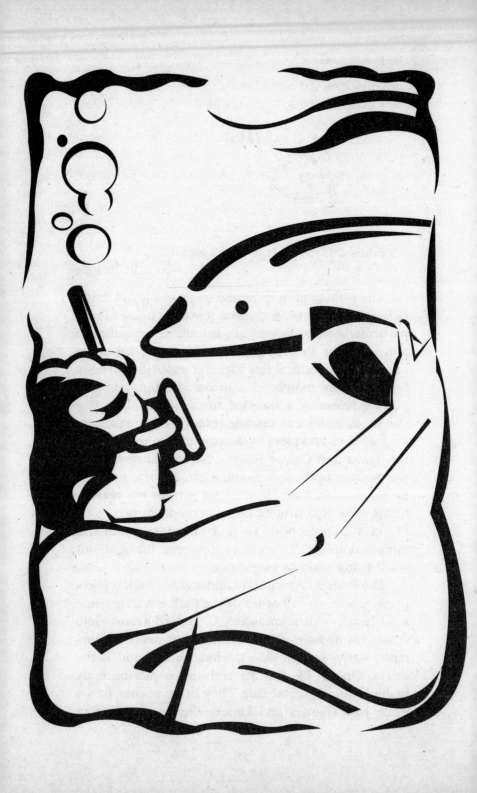

under them. To see kids flying through the air beyond the pier is a sure sign that Jojo is in a playful
mood.

Because of all this human activity there are some
who worry for Jojo's well-being. Yet, how do you re-
alistically protect a wild animal without restricting its
freedom?

The source of this dilemma is not long in arriving
at the bow of our charter vessel *Island Diver*. I thought
that Jojo, like most wild dolphins, would ride the bow
wave of our boat; instead he disappears beneath the
stern. Bill Rattey, the captain of *Island Diver*, slows the
engines. "You're not going to believe what Jojo is
doing right now," the captain says with a grin.

Intrigued, I don a face mask and flippers, then
slip over the side. *Island Diver* has two large propellers, each almost three feet in diameter. Incredibly,
Jojo is boldly swimming between the spinning propellers, dashing from one to the other, hovering just
inches from the swirling blades. I instantly understand
people's fears for the survival of this crazy dolphin.

When I return to the surface for a breath of air,
Captain Bill shouts, "Playing with spinning propellers
is not the only dangerous thing Jojo does, he also likes
to play chicken with ski boats."

Jojo suddenly surfaces next to me and chirps happily.

"He also enjoys knocking over novice skiers, which
probably explains that scar over his left eye," Bill adds
cheerfully.

Feeling a sharp nudge in the small of my back, I
spin about. Jojo is smiling as he backs away; it is the
kind of smile that lures me to play.

"He loves to play tag," Bill says with a grin, "but
you'll never catch him."

I lunge at Jojo, who twitters happily, then circles

me twice at warp velocity before diving out of sight.
Taking a deep breath, I plunge in pursuit. Swimming
downward at my maximum speed of about 3 MPH, I
am an easy target for the torpedoing dolphin. He
charges at 30 MPH plus, feigns left, then does a twisting backflip that results in a soft touch in the center
of my back.

Fifteen minutes later, I'm floating exhausted on
the surface with my tired legs hanging like wet noodles.
Jojo is five feet away daring me to catch him with
shrill squeaks and twitters. Suddenly, there is an abrupt
splash as something is thrown into the water. Glancing up, I see one of our underwater scooters floating
several feet away. Michel DeLoire, our cinematographer, is grinning from the back of the boat.

"Maybe that will even the odds a bit," Michel offers with a smile.

An underwater scooter looks and works exactly
like a miniature torpedo. I grab the handles, then face
Jojo, who is chirping confidently about ten feet away.
Jamming the accelerator to maximum, I shoot straight
at the elusive dolphin.

Jojo's shock is obvious as he sees me hurling towards him at three times human swimming speed. I
reach out and almost touch Jojo, but, at the last second, he goes ballistic—straight up. Jojo rockets completely out of the water, does a forward flip, and
comes down behind me. It's impossible to shake that
fast approaching nose. I dodge right, then do a quick
left wing over and shoot for the bottom. A rubbery
muzzle taps my back twice, then twice more, just so I
know who is really the master of this game.

We spend an incredible month capturing Jojo's
playful personality on film. In all that time, no matter
how hard I tried, I could never touch that crazy dolphin—that is, until the last day of the expedition.

Jojo and I are resting beneath the stern of the boat. I have just lost another extended game of tag. The scooter, its battery packs completely worn out, now hangs tethered to the boat. Jojo is floating in front of me just beyond arm's reach. He is making soft, restive clicking noises. He looks so tired, I begin to hum him a lullaby in my best Mickey Mouse voice. Jojo seems to like the high-pitched sound and inches a little closer.

Instantly, I want to touch him, but don't. This is a very special moment, and I do not want to frighten him away. Though Jojo loves people, he knows to be leery. Earlier this year, a teen-ager purposefully dropped a lit cigarette into Jojo's blow hole. It is hard for me to imagine that someone would do something so cruel to such a wonderful and unique creature. Yet, I also wonder why kids shoot each other with guns. It is the number two killer of children in America. So, I remain very still, humming the Disney theme song. Then, Jojo does a very amazing thing. He edges closer, softly nuzzles his muzzle under my arm, and goes to sleep.

Dolphins don't sleep like most mammals. Since they must surface to breath and always be alert for sharks, they swim very slowly with one eye closed while half of their brain sleeps at a time.

With the sleeping dolphin in my arms, I swim a few feet to the surface where he can breath effortlessly. Momentarily, both of Jojo's eyes look at me, then he offers a trusting smile, and the eyes slowly close together.

Floating in the calm water with a sleeping dolphin in my arms, I watch the red orb of the sun sink into the sea as the passionate colors of the sunset play in a wet reflection on his back. Slowly, the twilight fades to darkness, bringing out a multitude of twinkling stars. On the horizon, a crescent moon washes a fleet of clouds with its pale lunar light. Despite the tropical warmth of the water, I shiver slightly. Jojo stirs and opens his eyes. I softly rub under his chin as Jojo chirps his appreciation, then taking a deep breath he dives downward. His descending passage excites the phosphorescence in the water which fills his wake with sparkling blue light. Like a streaking comet, I watch the fiery wake arching off into the distance, then the phosphorescent trail, like the fading twinkle of pixy dust, dims to darkness, and I am alone in the dark water.

My excitement is hard to contain as I climb onto the boat to call my wife Cindy on the ship-to-shore telephone to tell her that a wild dolphin had actually fallen asleep in my arms.

"That's impossible," exclaims Cindy in utter astonishment. "No wild animal could put its nose in your smelly armpit and go to sleep."

The next day, I am sitting in a window seat of our departing plane. As the aircraft banks over the tiny island, I see what looks like a dolphin shadow slipping up behind a novice water skier. Beyond the unsuspecting skier, the turquoise waters of the Caribbean ocean extend as far as the eye can see.

I think that one of the wonders about Jojo is his unlimited freedom. He can go outside the dolphin norm to choose human friends as he desires and can live anywhere he likes—even off the end of a pier at a busy Caribbean dive resort.

We too are incredibly lucky in that freedom shines in America. We are free to worship God as we please, and our fortunes and adventures are only limited by our imaginations.

> Blessed is the nation whose God is the Lord,
> the people he chose for his inheritance. (Ps. 33:12)

Ours is a land that favors bold, inquisitive people with high hopes and aspirations. The challenge is simply to reach out and attempt to touch our dreams.

> *There are those, I know who will reply that the liberation of humanity, the freedom of man and mind is nothing but a dream. They are right, it is the American dream.* (Archibal Macleise)

Eleven

Pride goes before destruction, a haughty spirit before a fall.

—Proverbs 16:18

The steel shark cage hits the sand bottom hard, bounces upward two feet, and slams back into the sea bed before dragging to a stop tilting slightly to the left. Ten seconds later, the second cage crashes into the ocean floor driving its occupants half to their knees. A rising cloud of silt from the dual impacts is quickly swept away by a two-knot tidal current. Jean-Michel Cousteau grins from the other cage, then signals that all is OK. We are again in the realm of the great white shark.

David, a photographer standing to next me, looks to ensure there are no sharks about, then steps out of the cage, and promptly walks twenty feet across the bottom. Michel DeLoire and Capkin (our newest diver), step out from the other cage and begin examining the sea bed. They are looking for oysters and crabs for tonight's dinner.

Grocery shopping underwater is one of the advantages of being a diver—except for those of us who happen to be vegetarians. So, instead of dinner patrol, I'm on shark guard duty. With only a fifteen-minute bottom-time, we don't really expect to see any sharks—so of course, one arrives.

I see the massive shark coming; he swims rapidly out of the gloom. The shark is behind and slightly above the other divers, which is why they do not see him. Underwater, it is impossible to yell a warning. "Look out, shark!" I shout uselessly into my regulator.

Without realizing it, I step out of the cage and race towards my friends. Underwater, race is a relative term. Since we did not anticipate swimming, none of us are wearing flippers. Swim fins are a hindrance in a shark cage, where divers need to be weighted extra heavy for stability. Wearing two belts of lead, I move ponderously as I rush across the sea bed to warn my friends.

Meanwhile, the shark is heading towards David, who is completely unaware of the danger. He is taking pictures of Jean-Michel, who abruptly notices my awkward charge across the sand bottom. Instantly, Jean-Michel's face plate shifts towards the approaching shark.

Luckily, this is not an attack run. The shark, which is probably more curious than hungry, veers to one side as I reach out and grab David. The sudden contact causes him to spin about fearfully. Seeing me, he starts to relax—then David beholds the shark. He needs no further encouragement as he races for the security of the shark cage, so I go in pursuit of the other two divers, who are chasing spider crabs.

The shark continues to circle as I alert Capkin, then Michel DeLoire. In the ensuing shuffle, somehow I wind up being the last one outside the cages. The nearest cage already has three divers in it. Twenty feet away, I see my cage door standing open with David waiting inside. Instantly, I make one of the most foolish decisions of my life.

I begin to run toward the distant cage—against the tidal current. Plowing aggressively into the oncoming water flow, I move slowly forward at a mere 1 MPH. Having lost track of the shark, I worry it is heading directly at my exposed back. "Why didn't I just get into the closer cage?" I think furiously to myself. "Because you didn't want them to think you cowardly," my mind answers.

Time seems to slow as I focus on each forward step. "Idiot," I chastise myself, "you're making this frightening journey strictly because of social fear."

I am two steps from the open door when a dark shadow passes overhead. Believing the shark is on the verge of attacking, I lunge forward and dive into the cage, then anxiously turn to see empty water. On the surface, the *Alcyone* swings in the wind, casting a wandering shadow that now slowly moves away. The shark is nowhere to be seen.

Leaning against the cage wall trying to catch my breath, I think about the foolishness of my open run for the distant cage. How silly, to risk my life over concerns for what people may think of me.

Yet, this is a common human mistake; we often make poor choices trying to live up to other's expectations. In little leagues, kids live in terror of losing in front of their parents. The fear of embarrassment can be overpowering for a young person (over the last ten years, teen suicide has gone up by 700 percent). Teenage girls unintentionally get pregnant because they are conned into believing they must prove their love (a recent government report claims 40 percent of all teen-age girls will get pregnant before they turn twenty-years-old). Peer pressure is an awesome power that can shove a person into making a terrifying choice. Yet, when a friend dares us to do something dangerous or wrong, are they showing any concern for our well-being? Are they really being a friend?

There is only one whose expectations we should focus on, and that is Jesus Christ. He doesn't expect us to hit a ball further, nor does He care if we are short or tall. He simply wants to be our best friend and desires that we love our fellow man. These are expectations that lead us to happier, more satisfying lives.

> *For my yoke is easy and my burden is light.* (Matt. 11:30)

Twelve

Do not be misled: Bad company corrupts good character.

—1 Corinthians 15:33

It is three hours before sunset as the Cousteau windship *Alcyone* drops anchor at King's Cascade. It has taken us the entire morning and most of the afternoon to navigate the treacherous waters of the Prince Regent River in the remote Western Australia Territory. Standing on deck, I survey the quiet bay about us and listen to the cascading waterfalls that spill several hundred feet over numerous mossy ledges before splashing into the water just a few yards from our starboard side. The cool mist that floats heavily in the air is a welcome relief from the muggy heat of the Australian summer. Glancing at the outside thermometer, I see it is 102 degrees Fahrenheit, down from the noon high of 114 degrees.

The waterfalls look so refreshing, I desperately have to fight back the urge to dive into the cool water. Beside the cascading water, bold red letters crudely painted on the mist-covered rocks declare, "Danger, No Swimming. . . ." Wiping the sweat from my brow, I think about the young American actress who disregarded this warning barely two-months-ago.

Jessica (name changed) had always known she would be an actress. Even as a pre-teen, she usually

managed to get the lead role in her school and church plays. Then, one day something magical happened. She was selected from hundreds of other hopefuls for a part in a television situation comedy. Success and fortune came rapidly.

At the age of nineteen, Jessica allowed herself a well-earned vacation to Australia and even brought along her childhood girlfriend. The two lively girls met a couple of local Australian guys, who had a boat. They brought the girls here to King's Cascade. It was, as usual, extremely hot on that spring day, and the guys offered the two young women a couple of beers. They refused. Yet, the young Australian men were insistent, and besides, the cooler only contained beer.

Because it was so hot, the two girls chose to have more than a single beer. Soon, they began behaving recklessly, and abruptly, despite the warning cries of the two young men, they decided to jump into the water. The Australians urgently tried to call the girls back to the boat, but they laughed and swam for the rocks at the base of the waterfall. Jessica almost made it.

Standing on the *Alcyone*, I again read the warning painted in red on the rocks, "Danger, No Swimming, Crocodiles." The terror for the girls must have been horrifying, I think to myself.

On that beautiful spring day, Jessica's young life abruptly ended in a horrendous way as a huge crocodile took her just yards from the safety of the rocks. The other girl barely managed to scramble to safety as her childhood friend disappeared forever beneath the swirling water.

To one side of the cascade, I see two crocodiles on an exposed rock and shake my head sadly at the futility of such a senseless death. Alcohol and drunken activity are the number one killers of teen-agers.

> Do not join those who drink too much wine or
> gorge themselves on meat, for drunkards and
> gluttons become poor, and drowsiness clothes
> them in rags. (Prov. 23:20-22)

Christians must be strong in their beliefs and
commitments. Too often, young lives are prematurely
snuffed out because they do not stand up for what
they know is right. We should not allow others to dare
us into making bad choices. True adventures are for
sober people who are serious about enjoying life.

> Be careful, or your hearts will be weighed down
> with dissipation, drunkenness and the anxieties
> of life, and that day will close on you unexpect-
> edly like a trap. (Luke 21:34)

Thirteen

The world would be a very lonely place without our animal friends.

—Captain Jacques Y. Cousteau

Drifting in a Zodiac under a miserably hot Mexican sun, I wish for the relief of a cooling breeze. But, there isn't even a breath of air movement. The water is perfectly flat, except for the slight ripples where I last saw Murphy. He is free-diving with his camera, looking for photographic opportunities. Trying to hide under the minimal shade of my ball cap and a wet towel, I am anxious to get back to the air-conditioned comfort of our charter boat. It is anchored in a shaded harbor at nearby Socorro Island (three hundred miles south of Baja, Mexico). Unfortunately, I will probably be out here for a long time. Once Murphy gets in the water, there is no getting him out. As a marine scientist, he finds even the most mundane things extremely interesting.

Glancing at my watch, I see Murf has been down for just over a minute. That means he should be up in about thirty seconds for three or four breathes of air before disappearing again. Abruptly, Murf erupts chest-high out of the water, both arms waving urgently, and yelling through his snorkel. I jerk the outboard's pull start, shift to forward, and jam the throttle wide open. The Zodiac leaps forward. Murphy

is turning in place, looking straight down into the water. His posture is so obviously defensive, I don't doubt he is confronting a predator. Coming alongside Murphy, I cut the engine and quickly reach out to grab him, but Murf doesn't need any help getting into the boat. He launches himself up and over the side of the boat landing face down on the floor boards with a solid face-smacking thud.

Looking quickly down into the water, I see two torpedo-like shapes disappearing back down into the depths. "What kind of sharks are they, Murf?" I tease, keeping my voice purposefully casual.

"Hungry, they are hungry sharks!" Murphy is gasping for air as he adds, "Meanest Galapagos sharks I've ever seen."

I am surprised. "Galapagos sharks are aggressive?"

"These ones are." Murphy begins checking his camera. "I got to get some pictures of them; this is pretty wild behavior for Galapagos sharks."

"You're going back into the water?" I ask in complete surprise.

"Yeah," Murphy smiles, "with your help."

A few minutes later Murphy is indeed back in the water, at least the top half of him is. His legs are still in the boat. I have tied the anchor line—minus the anchor of course—around his chest, and now I am in a ready position above him. If he starts thrashing or screaming through his snorkel, it is the pre-arranged signal for me to jerk him up—which takes all of about thirty seconds.

"Forget it." Murphy is again face down on the floor boards. "I'm not going back in," he says, untying the rope from his chest. "These sharks are just too aggressive."

After stowing Murphy's camera, we are soon heading back for our charter boat. I am daydreaming about lounging under the air conditioner when a huge dark shape passes under our bow.

"Giant manta ray," Murphy shouts excitedly.

Instantly, I throttle back the Zodiac and grab my fins. "My turn?" I ask hopefully. For the past couple of days, we have been taking turns catching rides on the giant, but friendly, manta rays.

"Go for it," Murf replies with a grin.

Hurling myself into the water, I race after the ray. The manta has a wing spread of twelve feet or more. Except for a gentle turn to check me out, the big ray is undisturbed by my presence. I quickly close and latch onto the leading edge of her mid-body. Sensing my abrupt added weight, the manta increases speed to shake me off, which is where the fun really begins. Unlike riding a horse, which mostly only goes forward, riding a manta ray is like latching onto a giant bird—a bird that flies underwater.

The manta does a shallow dive, banks to the right, then goes into a tight left vertical spin. I'm hoping she heads back for the surface soon so I can get another breath of air, when I notice something flash by off to my left. A quick glance confirms my worst fear—it is a shark about seven feet long. A threatening shadow lurking twenty feet below me turns out to be the shark's bigger brother. A fast look back over my shoulder confirms the inflatable is getting further away. I have no choice but to let go of the manta, which is pleased to be rid of me. She dives down towards the depths, while I swim rapidly upward. I break the surface, arms waving and shouting for Murphy, who quickly responds.

Sticking my face back into the water, I see the sharks swimming about fifteen feet beneath me. Only instead of two, there is now a small group. They are darting about, which is not a good sign. Then I hear the muffled roar of the outboard as Murf arrives. It takes about a micro-second to launch myself out of the shark-infested water and into the safety of the boat.

I am still face down on the floor boards panting when Murphy leans over and casually asks, "Galapagos sharks?"

"It looks like a shark express pool down there," I answer between pants.

"There must not be very much for them to eat." Murf is now in his scientist mode. Lately, he has been doing research on the tragic levels of over-fishing in Baja, Mexico. The fishermen here often use outdated techniques for catching fish and shrimp. Huge nets, up to a mile long, capture a diversity of fish and other marine life. The commercial fish go into the ship's hold, but a wealth of non-marketable fish and other marine creatures (like dolphins) are also caught, however, their remains are just shoveled over the side like so much trash. Even worse are the commercial shrimpers; they use bottom scraping machines that completely uproot the fertile sea bed in pursuit of a few tiny crustaceans. The result of this extremely destructive type of harvesting leaves a lot less marine life in these waters than there used to be, and it is getting rapidly worse on a global scale.

"Maybe it's revenge, Murf," I offer.

"Yeah, against the shark fishermen," Murphy replies. "They are the most evil of the whole bunch."

Some of the more greedy fishermen have resorted to taking sharks strictly for their fins. In Asia, there is a big demand for shark fins to make soup. Some oriental people believe that eating shark-fin soup makes them healthier and stronger. Unfortunately, this ancient belief is bad news for sharks.

Earlier in the expedition, we had seen a commercial shark fishing boat at work. They catch the sharks on long lines from which dangle a series of baited hooks. As the sharks are hauled onto the deck, one man hits them with a club to stun them, then another rapidly cuts off their fins. The maimed, still living sharks are then kicked back into the ocean to die a slow and painful death.

It is amazing to think that man's greed permits him to be so cruel. Yet, sharks are not the only victims of outdated beliefs that promote the eating of exotic animal parts for their supposed healing properties. In our national parks, illegal hunters kill bears for their paws and gall bladders, which are turned into oriental remedy foods. In Africa, poachers kill rhinoceroses strictly for their horns and tigers for their claws to feed these same ridiculous superstitions.

Most of the problems of the world always seem to come back to man's greed and his lack of caring. Right now, it appears that it is the animals who are suffering the most, but unless we change our ways it is the human race that will in the end pay the highest price.

From the least to the greatest, all are greedy for gain.
(Jer. 6:13)

Fourteen

It is for freedom that Christ has set us free. Stand firm, then, and do not let yourselves be burdened again by a yoke of slavery.

—Galatians 5:1

There is a tiny island in the Central Pacific Ocean that was once so beautiful the old sailing captains called it Pleasant Island. Lush with tropical foliage and full of healthy vibrant people, it was a favorite stop to replenish water and food supplies. Pleasant Island is now known as Nauru, and, like its name, the island has changed.

The Cousteau Windship *Alcyone* arrives at Nauru Island just after sunrise. A thundercloud falls off to the east after thoroughly wetting the squat tropical island. The green shoreline gives no hint of the wealth that lies hidden from our sight on the upper plateau of the island. The five thousand inhabitants of this remote island community are (per capita) among the richest people in the world, but they are very unhappy.

It is on the plateau where our journey begins . . .

Standing in the shade of a dense canopy of a rain forest, I stare in awe at a towering coral pinnacle over twenty feet tall. Encasing the ancient coral are the standing roots of a giant Banyan tree. I touch the tree's smooth trunk, then look upwards into its vast

canopy. From its many branches hangs a cascading tapestry of green vines with fragrant white flowers. At my feet, the tree's gnarled roots disappear into dark fertile soil that is blanketed with green moss and soft dichondra. Standing in the beauty of this tiny Eden, I regretfully listen to the horrible mechanical sound of engines consuming the last of this rain forest.

Only a hundred feet away, giant shovels and tractors strip away the forest and topsoil to get at the valuable phosphate below. The once majestic tree trunks are stripped and stacked for later sale, while the rest of the forest's foliage is dumped in a heap to rot in the sun. In a few days, the ancient towering Banyan tree standing majestically before me, along with this little piece of rain forest, will be gone forever.

The phosphate is the source of the Nauruan's wealth and problems. Phosphate is the third most traded commodity in the world. The phosphate (bird droppings and microscopic marine organisms) was laid down eons ago when Nauru was still a growing atoll. For over a century, the export of phosphate has made the tiny island nation incredibly rich—and extremely land poor.

The topsoil which once supported crops and a vast rain forest is 90 percent gone. The people have nowhere left to live but a narrow coastal fringe. Food and water must now be imported at great expense. Even though the government has invested a huge sum of money for the near future, when the phosphate is gone, that money will not last. Because of greed, these people are selling their children and their future generations into a monetary slavery. It is a yoke the people are placing around their own necks. The choices are already made and beyond changing.

Even the seemingly endless resources of the ocean are under stress. The once picturesque coral reefs around the island are rapidly dying.

Diving the island's reefs is like visiting an underwater cemetery—a cemetery that has been grossly neglected. Small isolated patches of living coral are surrounded by broad areas of dead and decaying coral that are bleached white like exposed bones. Whole coral shelves lie smothered under a death shroud of sediment and phosphate dust from which protrudes broken coral fingers laced with long webs of dark filamentous algae. Lacking living coral, the reef is all but empty of fish. Once a garden of underwater life, the reefs are swiftly becoming barren submarine deserts.

The rain that falls on the island is no longer slowed or contained by a layer of vegetation and soil. This freshwater flushing coats the reefs with excessive minerals and changes the reef's salinity. Another reason why the reefs are dying is actually part of a greater world-wide problem—global warming. Coral reefs around the world are under stress or dying because of equatorial ocean warming.

As *Alcyone* prepares to leave this unhappy place, we suit up to make a final open water night dive. Descending into the cool dark water, the bright glare of our camera lights reveals numerous macroscopic creatures. The ocean about us is so full of miniature life it is like swimming through a cosmic soup. We film transparent jellyfish no bigger than a thumbnail, each resembling miniature lighter-than-air balloons with filamentous stripes running along their sides that electrically pulsate in a luminous glow. Some of the tiny gelatinous creatures drift with the tide, others swim slowly like the winged pteropods that resemble Darth Vader's starship, while even smaller creatures

flick about in rapid spinning circles like errant miniature skyrockets. We are at a foundation level of the
world's food chain, and it is here that the impact of
world pollution will first be felt.

Nauru is a remote island in a huge ocean, yet what
happens here may well be a precursor for island earth
floating in a vast universe.

> How many are your works, O Lord! In wisdom
> you made them all; the earth is full of your
> creatures. There is the sea, vast and spacious,
> teeming with creatures beyond number—living
> things both large and small. There the ships go
> to and fro, and the leviathan, which you formed
> to frolic there. (Ps. 104:24–34)

If we love God, we should respect and take care
of his creations. If we love our fellow man, we need
to become personally involved in making this world,
our home, a better place for all of us to live.

Fifteen

Most people are about as happy as they make up their minds to be.

—Abraham Lincoln

At five o'clock in the morning, the stern of the *Alcyone* is cast in darkness except for the dancing light coming from Antoine's flashlight. While I warm up the outboard engine on the Zodiac, Capkin carefully loads our gear into the inflatable boat. It is not unusual for us divers to be up so early, however it is not a working dive we are preparing for. Capkin grins as he carefully lays the three surfboards down. "This is going to be a lot of fun," he declares rubbing his hands together in eager anticipation.

Peering through a pair of binoculars, I can barely see the waves at the distant reef, but it looks like major surf. All I can see in the darkness are fast-moving lines of white water reflecting soft lunar light from a full moon riding low on the horizon. "Looks big, maybe eight- to ten-foot faces." My enthusiasm is hard to contain.

Antoine chuckles as he jumps into the Zodiac. Untying the bow and giving us a push off, he turns and says in an excited voice, "Light offshore winds, those waves are going to be like glass walls."

In sync with our growing excitement, I twist the outboard's throttle "to the max." The lightly-loaded

Zodiac leaps forward and rapidly accelerates to full plane. At 30 MPH, the outboard roars with the Zodiac skimming across the smooth water. Antoine stands at the front of the racing boat balancing himself with the bowline. Leaving the harbor, I hug the coastline of this beautiful Fijian island. In the darkness, we pass white sand and seashell laced beaches that twinkle; it is bits of white shells reflecting the silver lunar light. Where the beach meets the jungle there is a small seaside village. Through the rectangular windows of the huts there are soft flickering glows from open fires where breakfast will soon be prepared. At the harbor point, a dog runs down to the water's edge to bark at us as we go by. Before us, the distant horizon is just beginning to lighten, heralding the advance of the tropical sunrise.

Angling out to sea, the Zodiac flies over the beginnings of an ocean swell, which is increasing in magnitude. Soon the sleek inflatable is momentarily airborne as it launches off a sizable cresting swell. Antoine rides at the bow with his knees flexed shouting for more speed.

Fifteen minutes later, we arrive at the reef. The surf is bigger than expected, at least double-overhead. Barely twenty-five feet from the breaking waves, we drop anchor in the protection of a deep water channel. Quickly pulling on our rubber vests, we grab our surfboards and leap into the warm water. As we are paddling out, the rim of the rising sun crests the horizon. Warm yellow light washes across the glassy wave faces.

Capkin, who has the advantage of youth and long arms on a six-foot, five-inch frame is the first one out into the line-up. He quickly drops into a twelve-foot face screaming his lungs out. When the wave passes beside us, he momentarily disappears from sight as he races down its face, then he arches back up slicing the lip and throwing a wide fan of water over us. The water particles sparkle in the morning light, and for an instant there are twin miniature rainbows caught in the misty arch.

Antoine attempts the next wave. An inexperienced surfer, he is unsure of himself and is too far forward on the board. The wave launches him face first into the water, then he and his board disappear into the frothy surf.

A couple of seconds later, I am paddling for my own wave. Feeling the board begin to fall and accelerate with the wave, I leap to my feet. The surfboard surges forward. Shifting weight to my rear foot, the board angles up at the bottom of the wave and races across the glassy face. Through the clean wall of water, I can see the fiery red and yellow orb of the sun as it burnishes the wave in the glorious colors of the sunrise. Reaching out, I trail my hand in the smooth wave face and stare in awe at light and water rippling off my fingertips like spinning liquid fire. Behind me, I hear the roaring sound of the wave pounding the shallow reef, then the wave crest drops over my shoulder. In an instant, I am inside a glassy tube, a rolling vortex of water with shimmering liquid walls. I can see the mouth of the wave closing before me, then abruptly the wave's lip, like a hydraulic sledgehammer, slams me from the board. Tumbling and spinning, I hurl underwater mere feet above the shallow reef. Finally reaching the surface, gasping for air, I hear Capkin laughing a few feet away.

"You looked terrific," he shouts in glee, "right up till that wave swallowed you, then spit out your board like a chewed-up tooth pick."

Laughing together, we turn to see Antoine's next attempt. It is a nice wave, only Antoine is too far back on the board. Waving his arms in frustration, he falls over backwards, his feet disappearing last into the froth. Several seconds later, the wave washes him and his board to where we are waiting. He comes up sputtering and spitting water.

"You're trying to stand up too fast," offers Capkin. "Let the board gather speed, and it will be more stable."

"If I want any advice from a beginner, I'll ask for it," Antoine responds angrily.

Capkin shrugs and leads the way as we paddle out for the next set. It is true that Capkin has the least experience of the three of us, yet already I know he is a natural for the sport. Despite his awkward style, he rides well and aggressively.

Over the next hour, Capkin rips wave after wave. I catch less than half as many and often wind up in the underwater subway bouncing along the bottom; but Antoine doesn't catch any at all. Soon, he is furious, sometimes pounding the water in frustration. Neither Capkin nor I spend much time around him. Half an hour later, we are back in the Zodiac returning towards *Alcyone*. Capkin and I are in nonexpressed good moods because Antoine is so angry with himself and life in general. Back at the windship, he tosses his surfboard onto the deck and goes below.

How foolish, I think to myself. Antoine's poor performance was a direct reflection of his attitude. We went surfing to have fun, yet he wanted none of our cheerfulness because of his lousy attitude and inability to catch a wave. I don't doubt that his anger interfered with his surfing. Had he relaxed and not worried about how he looked in front of his friends, all of us would have had a better time. The Bible states this very well:

Get rid of all bitterness, rage and anger, brawl-
ing and slander, along with every form of malice.
(Eph. 4:31)

Anger, even when it is self-directed, steals happiness, upsets friends, and ruins potentially happy times.
There is absolutely no benefit in being mad—except
for the negative lessons it teaches us about ourselves.

Capkin and I are rinsing off our surfboards when
Jean-Michel Cousteau steps out on deck. "We won't
be getting underway this morning after all," he announces sadly. "Customs hasn't cleared our permit
yet."

Capkin and I look at each other as wide grins slop
across our faces.

"What are you two so happy about?" inquires Jean-
Michel, who wants to go diving in the worst way. We
are in Fiji to investigate a deep underwater cave.

"Well boss," I say as Capkin and I stand hopefully
holding our surfboards, "the waves are really good
right now."

Jean-Michel eyes us sternly, "Have you two no-
ticed that the bridge needs a good scrubbing?"

"I could do it during lunchtime," volunteers
Capkin. This is a major concession from him because
Capkin is always hungry. Often, he raids the refrigerator late at night much to the frustration of our French
chef. Lately, the chef has taken to hiding certain things
like cooking chocolate from Capkin. The chef's ef-
forts are mostly wasted as Capkin considers the hunt
for hidden treats to be almost as much fun as eating
them.

"Na," grins Jean-Michel, "you two go have fun.
Antoine is in a bit of a mood in the galley right now.
Maybe a little work will improve his attitude."

Learn the sweet magic of a cheerful face. (Oliver
Wendell Holmes)

Sixteen

Even in laughter the heart may ache, and joy may end in grief.

—Proverbs 14:13

The bow of the Zodiac lifts dramatically as a wave rolls over the shallow reef. At the inflatable's bow, twin anchor lines go taut, resisting the surging water. Around us we see only the ocean. There are no landmarks to identify this submerged reef in Fiji's outer islands, which is fortunate because we are about to make a very dangerous dive. Deep below us lies an underwater cave that has taken the lives of four very talented divers. It is best if its location is kept secret.

Donning my mask, I make a last check to ensure the Zodiacs are well anchored and will not be washed back onto the reef. I nod to the other Cousteau divers, then silently slip over the side right after a large foaming wave. The rolling water surges with bubbles as I rapidly kick downwards and grab onto a coral pentacle to stabilize myself against the strong undertow. When the entire team of five is present, we swim to the edge of the shelf, then quickly descend down a vertical wall of multicolored coral. The reef wall is a hanging marine garden that plunges hundreds of feet straight down to the ocean floor far below. We pass close to a large orange sea fan folding and unfolding in the current with a red gorgonian clinging tena-

ciously to its swaying branches. At sixty feet, we swim
by a yellow-banded clownfish nuzzling against an elec-
tric blue sea anemone that is its protector and home.
Deeper and deeper we descend, where the reef's passionate colors slowly dull, and their rich hues mutate
from vibrant reds and brilliant yellows to dark greens
and deep blues.

At a hundred feet, the water turns sharply colder,
yet we hardly notice as we race downward. This will
be a very deep dive, and our bottom time will be
severely limited. The pressure compresses our wet
suits, thus reducing our buoyancy and increasing the
speed of our descent into the dim twilight of deep
water. At one hundred and forty feet, I see the dark
opening of the cave lurking below—instantly I feel a
chill of dread and anticipation. At one hundred and
sixty-five feet, we reach the cave's craggy mouth and,
as we swim hesitantly inside, are immediately swallowed by a foreboding darkness.

One after another, the divers switch on their lights.
Bright beams of pale light play haphazardly on the
cave's narrowing walls throwing sharp-edged shadows
that drift with our passage. There are no signs of life
on the bare rock, but for the dark smear of algae
patches and the occasional lobster sentinel peering
from dark crevices. The cave sides constrict to a small
throat—it is here that we encounter the first whale
skull.

No one really knows why this family of four pilot
whales died here, or even when, because the bones
are fossilized. The drama could have played itself out
thousands of years ago, yet the empty sockets staring
from the bleached skull still depict the tragedy and
loss that occurred in this dark underwater grave. This,
the largest skull, is probably the father, a mute guard
to what waits within. For a brief moment, I wonder if

the family of whales fled inside the cave while the father turned to face a fierce predator.

Slowly, we continue our dark journey inward. The walls continue to close in as the cave now leads slowly upwards into a small cavern. The second skull appears suddenly, resting on a bed of white sand. A flicker of movement inside the staring skull startles me, then I realize it is just a tiny red fish fleeing our lights.

This is where the mother died. She had enough room to turn around and, like her mate, could have swam out, but apparently chose not to. The answer, I believe, waits above us through a narrow chimney of stone. Carefully, I climb upwards, weaving my way through the sharp confining rock. My air tanks catch several times, and I feel my wetsuit snag and tear. Cold water rushes into my suit, yet I do not know if the chill that runs down my spine is from the chilly water or the fear of apprehension for what I am about to see. Finally, I reach the top of the chimney and the end of the cave. I am two hundred and fifty feet into the foundation of the reef. Here, inside a tiny crypt, are two small skulls lying among a clutter of bones on a slender ledge. The skulls are side by side, as if still seeking mutual security—this is where the two young whales died.

Staring at the ghostly remains, I am sure that it was no threatening predator that drove this family into the cave. Rather, I believe it was the curiosity of the two young whales at play. Discovering the cave's broad mouth they probably swam inside to investigate a potential mystery. But, as the walls constricted they could only swim forward. At the small inner chamber, they encountered the cramped shaft of the chimney that led upwards. Their instincts would tell them that up leads to the surface and potentially to air. Fighting their way through the tight stone passage, they arrived at a dead end where there just was not enough room for them to turn around.

The parents probably could not resist following their children into the dark trap. The father's bulk stopped him just inside the entrance, whereas the mother managed to squeeze all the way into the inner chamber. Though the parents should have been able to swim out, I think they chose not to. Listening to the fading cries of their children, they had no choice but to stay, and that I think is how the family of four died.

As we live our lives, pursuing our hopes, goals, and aspirations, we must remember that death is always stalking us and those we love. Life cannot be lived frivolously. Tragedy lurks around every corner. Yet, future tribulations also bear a very special gift of encouragement. A stimulus of love animates us to live as intensely as possible, to always seek out the newness and wonder of our short existence.

There is another lesson here, which lies in the powerful love of family and close friends. Love is a wonderful closeness that must be cherished and nourished. Since life is so fragile, we cannot allow the treasure of love to be clouded with needless anger and jealousies. We must always look to support our friends and loved ones, to be careful to part from others with feelings of goodwill, because none of us knows when or where tragedy will next take its frightful toll.

I loved my big brother Jim. As kids, he was always there to protect me. I remember how I worried when he went off to Vietnam; then, a year later it was his turn to worry as I went off to serve my country in that distant conflict. Between us, we made a total of six tours to that frightful land, yet we came home unharmed. The personal fears we shared bound us closer than most brothers. Each of us married and started families of our own. Responsibilities often kept us apart, which made our times together that much more cherished. We always parted with a hug, and that is how I will always remember him—smiling, as we stood, arms around each other's shoulders.

Last week, my brother died unexpectedly. He was young and full of health—then abruptly he was gone. In my heart, and in my future, there is a huge emptiness where a great loss now resides. Fortunately, I am at peace with my memories of Jim. Our love is a cement that keeps us together always. It is a love unclouded by regrets. It allows me to go on with my life while Jim now sleeps in the arms of the Lord.

Knowing true peace in life is not an easy task. It takes hard work and real awareness to make the most of our brief existence on this earth. We must treasure our lives and the lives of those around us, for no one knows what the future holds. Life is a mystery and security is easily wiped away.

> *Love is patient, love is kind. It does not envy, it does not boast, it is not proud. It is not rude, it is not self-seeking, it is not easily angered, it keeps no record of wrongs. Love does not delight in evil but rejoices with the truth. It always protects, always trusts, always hopes, always perseveres.* (1 Cor. 13:4–7)

Seventeen

Nature presents us with an infinite variety of attitudes—from gloomy mist to glorious sunshine. Our own moods, whether gloomy or bright, radiate to those around us.

—Unknown

Even on an expedition of adventure, sometimes there are days which can seem rather boring; this morning appears to be one of them. I am very uncomfortable in my rubber wetsuit sitting in an inflatable boat with the hot tropical sun of Papua New Guinea beating down on me. We are idling slowly through the water, looking for the mouth of a small cave in the reef below us. It is not much of a cave; it only goes back a few dozen feet. The mouth is very near the surface, where it is exposed to surge from wave action. That means the visibility will be poor, and I can look forward to being slammed regularly against the sharp rocks by abrupt onrushes of surf. Considering that we are here to film a small, almost blind fish that lives in the shallow cave does not add to my sense of adventure.

There is a slight breeze coming off the bow of the Zodiac. So, I'm looking in that direction to keep my face cool when a massive dorsal fin, four feet high, suddenly rises out of the water right in front of us.

"Orcas!" shouts Jean-Michel. "Stop the boat." Quickly donning a mask, he dunks his face into the

water. With his flippered feet sticking into the air, Jean-Michel looks a lot like a duck bottom-side-up. A moment later, he pulls back into the Zodiac. "There are three of them," he exclaims. "Forget the blind fishy, we're going after the whales."

My heart leaps with sudden anticipation. Stripping off my scuba tank (whales do not like a diver's bubbles), I take a deep breath and roll backwards into the warm water. The orcas immediately wheel back to investigate us small creatures with oddly bubbling heads. Realizing that we are pursuing one of the largest predators in the world is actually quite unnerving. Orcas are called killer whales because of their aggressive nature; nothing in the water is safe when they are present and hungry. Killer whales eat almost anything including seals, walruses, dolphins, other whales, and sharks. The only reason we can even get in the water with them is because orcas are not known for purposefully attacking people.

Ten feet beneath the Zodiac, the orcas circle us for several minutes. At first, the four of us divers stay in a tight group for emotional security. But soon, the whales return to their business of hunting for food, which leaves us swimming awkwardly in their wakes just trying to keep up.

The big male, about twenty-two feet long, surprises a large manta ray cruising in the shelter of the coral reef. Instantly, the whale spurts forward at about 30 MPH. The manta ray twists and rolls as it flees, but it doesn't have a chance. Three seconds and two bites later, there is no trace of the ray left—just empty blue water with a scar of red where a two hundred pound ray once was. Swimming just a dozen feet away, I am stunned by the sudden fierceness of the attack.

The bull orca hardly even notices me as he swims onward aggressively looking for more game. I subconsciously breathe a sigh of relief, then realize I am holding my breath and am short on air. I begin to swim toward the surface for a much needed breath. Turning as I swim, I abruptly see a female orca hovering behind me. She is only twenty-five feet away and staring right at me. I freeze in place as I see her tail begin moving slowly and powerfully, propelling the massive animal right in my direction. Desperately, I want to shoot upwards for the surface; instead I stare in fascination at the huge approaching predator. There is an abrupt loud clicking/popping noise as she directs a barrage of sound waves right at me. Orcas can see acoustically (with sound), which means she is aware that my heart is beating wildly. I consciously try to slow my heart down, but it continues to race in pace with my growing alarm.

I know if the killer whale decides to attack there is nothing I can do. She is barely a dozen feet away when she makes a slow, deliberate turn to one side and drifts to a stop. We are only separated by ten feet as I stare in awe at the wild intelligence regarding me. An orca's eye is actually quite small considering the size of the animal. I couldn't help wondering what she was thinking about. Did she know what humans are? Did she turn sideways to purposefully be less threatening? These thoughts are interrupted by my now urgent need for air. Unable to wait any longer, I quickly swim upwards for several much needed breaths. When I stick my head back into the water, the whale is gone.

Feeling very unnerved, I decide to head back to the Zodiac for a short rest.

"What are you doing?" asks Jean-Michel who surfaces at the side of the small inflatable.

"Resting," I respond.

"Really?" Jean-Michel isn't convinced. "You know," he continues as he climbs into the Zodiac, "before the whales arrived you were looking pretty bored."

"Yeah, I know," I answer, not sure where he is leading.

"I am never bored," he says with a grin. "Life is just too adventurous. Who could know what is going to happen next?"

I realize that Jean-Michel is saying something really important. Life is supposed to be exciting, unexpected, and mysterious. Every moment is a potential adventure waiting to unfold. Abruptly, I realize that a whale of an adventure is still somewhere beneath us. *What am I doing up here?* I think to myself.

A large splash announces that Jean-Michel is back in the water. On the surface, he readjusts his dive mask, then asks, "Aren't you coming?"

Quickly standing, I leap over the side.

> *Security is mostly a superstition. It does not exist in nature. . . . Life is either a daring adventure or nothing.* (Helen Keller)

Eighteen

Your beauty should not come from outward adornment, such as braided hair and the wearing of gold jewelry and fine clothes. Instead, it should be that of your inner self, the unfading beauty of a gentle and quiet spirit, which is of great worth in God's sight.

—1 Peter 3:3–4

Lounging in the shade of a coconut tree in Papua New Guinea, I watch island children playing in the sun. Actually, many of them are involved in work, yet, from their happy attitudes, one wouldn't know that this is labor. The boys, many accompanied by their fathers, are mostly fishing from canoes or mending nets. The girls, depending upon their age, are either helping their mothers make meals or are weaving baskets from coconut fronds. The younger children are at play in the water or chasing each other about the lush jungle foliage.

This village is located on one of Papua New Guinea's smaller islands, a lonely isolated outpost in the Indian Ocean. The villagers live simply in wooden huts with bamboo frond roofs. They are a happy people who take great pride in their surroundings. They regularly sweep the island's dirt paths and like to encourage flowering plants to grow around their doorways and windows.

Their needs are not complex. There is no electricity, radios, or television in the village. Kerosene lamps provide a soft evening glow for reading, and the flame's light smoke helps to keep the mosquitoes away. Money is almost nonexistent in this quiet society, except for the necklaces. The villagers' money necklaces are made from tiny seashells, about the size of a child's little fingernail. It takes the entire village a full day's labor to make just one money necklace. Only special shells of the right size and color will do; the children and adults comb the beaches and hunt underwater for them. Each shell is laboriously hand-sanded to a tiny oval, no bigger than a BB, then a hole is carefully bored into them with a primitive bow-like awl. In the evening, the women weave strands of their hair into fine cords on which they string the precious shells.

The resulting necklace has such great value it is given a special name. When two island chiefs meet in traditional ceremonies, they exchange money necklaces to the honor of each village. The necklaces are also one of the ways that the island parents show their children how important they are to them. When a young couple is to wed, the whole village contributes to their bridal dowry—usually thirty money necklaces or more.

Relaxing on the warm sand, I realize that it is rather easy for the village children to grasp their personal value and to understand their future place in this tiny island society.

Abruptly, a single loud horn blast puts an end to this relaxing moment bringing me to my feet. It is the signal that *Alcyone* is ready to get underway. We are leaving with the evening tide for Australia, to be followed by a two-month break in our round-the-world tour of discovery. I am looking forward to getting home and seeing Cindy, the girl I will soon marry.

Barely two weeks later, I am again relaxing under a tree—only this tree is made of plastic with artificial silk leaves. There is a small mechanical bird singing in its wire-reinforced branches. Cindy has left me unattended while she shops in a crowded California mall. Actually, I am somewhat in a state of shock. It is always rather startling to return from a remote expedition location to the crowded press of humanity choking the big cities of our modern society. Idly, I am mostly watching teen-agers. I wonder how many of them actually know where they are going or what they will do when they get there?

I think how different life is for these kids compared to the children of Papua New Guinea. For a youth on a tiny remote island, there are few options. The boys can fish and farm or learn a primitive trade. Most of the girls will become mothers and tend to their families as their age-old traditions dictate. Basically, that is the extent of their choices. Few, if any, of the island children will get an opportunity for an education or a chance to travel outside their tiny island sphere. For North American children, however, there are limitless choices. Armed with a broad knowledge of their modern world, they can choose from an incredible diversity of careers and opportunities. Realizing this, one would think that most kids are actively preparing themselves to go after their dreams and aspirations. Yet, sitting under the plastic tree with the mechanical bird singing, I see little evidence of this. From their dress, attitudes, and activities, I get clues on these particular teen-agers' potential futures.

Before me, a group of young people saunters into view. Half of them are smoking cigarettes, which unfortunately makes them early candidates for extensive health problems and assures a shortened and less dynamic life. The girls are apparently buying their make-up on sale by the pound. I see that green hair dye is in style—for one of the guys. Their jewelry is mostly cheap imitations of Nazi memorabilia, which is worn through the nose or in multiple assortments on either ear. Dirty leather and T-shirts decorated with skulls and copious amounts of blood are obviously popular with this morbid group.

They are discussing the merits of a headbanger band. Passing a video game shop, the group has to make room for a man coming from the opposite direction. He has horrible posture, poor personal hygiene, ragged clothes and the lack of alertness of someone who lives on the streets. He actually appears to fit in well with this group of kids. Seemingly, the youths think so, too. They are very impressed with a tattoo on the man's left arm. For a few moments, there is animated conversation as they discuss with him the artistic points of his "dead-head" tattoo. I thought it would be more productive for the man to give them a few points on being homeless because this group of youths is headed for "nowhere" occupations at warp speed—that is, unless they are inadvertently sidetracked to an extended stay at a prison or trip into an early plot in a graveyard.

Evidently, I am not alone in my observations. A pair of high school girls pauses under my plastic tree to stare at the headbangers as they shove into the game parlor.

"What a bunch of losers," observes a blond-haired girl. She is wearing an extremely low cut halter top and a skin-tight mini-skirt.

"Yeah," her friend answers, loudly cracking her gum, "real creeps for sure." She is at least fifty pounds overweight, so her form-fitting lycra bicycling suit gives me no reassurance that she actually likes to ride bikes.

The girls are glancing about regularly to see if

their provocative clothes are drawing any attention. "Want to go hang out at the record store?" asks the blond.

"Sure," her friend replies, "the clerk there is really cute."

The mechanical bird, though unappreciated, continues to sing as the girls start to leave. An instant later, they both pause abruptly. A guy is coming from the opposite direction. He is of an average height but looks taller because of his athletic physique and excellent posture. He is wearing a plain white shirt and jeans. He looks very likable.

"Hey, he goes to our school," exclaims the overweight girl.

"Yeah," chimes the blond, "but you never see him at the parties. He's one of those study freaks."

Her friend nods knowingly, "Let's go check out the clerk."

As the girls disappear up the mall, their heads swiveling, hoping to see if anyone is checking them out, I watch the guy go into a sporting goods store. Through a window, I see him enthusiastically trying on a back pack. There is no doubt in my mind that he is the happiest of the youths I have observed. If he studies hard, pursues adventure, and is content to just be himself while focusing on being a good person, then he has a good head start on a wonderful life.

For the other young people, I realize that it must be hard growing up in a busy modern society like America, where evaluating your self-worth can be confusing and outright disheartening. Living in a crush of humanity, teens and young children often find themselves alone—and seemingly unappreciated. In angry response, they may make some poor choices, even purposefully head in negative or wrong directions. Yet, even for the headbangers, there is hope. No one is ever completely lost. If someone makes a mistake, it doesn't mean that they are a mistake. Any of us can take our mistakes and all that we dislike about ourselves and give these burdens to the Lord—and He will give us a fresh new beginning.

> I have told you these things, so that in me you may have peace. In this world you will have trouble. But take heart! I have overcome the world. (John 16:33)

Jesus willingly suffered being nailed to a cross for you and for me. His love makes each of us incredibly valuable beyond any earthly measurement. Remember that none of us are ever alone or without value. There is no greater nor more loving friend than Jesus.

Nineteen

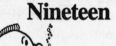

A keen sense of humor helps us to overlook the unbecoming, understand the unconventional, tolerate the unpleasant, overcome the unexpected, and outlast the unbearable.

—Billy Graham

Motoring in on the back of a small wave, our Zodiac nudges up against a seaweed-laced rock. Capkin and I leap ashore as the inflatable boat quickly backs away. We scurry up a rocky ledge to avoid the next set of waves, then pause to survey Dangerous Reef. We are in South Australian waters, taking a little time out during our Great White Shark Expedition to do a little sightseeing. A small pair of shy brown eyes curiously watching us from a ledge a little higher up is the object of this adventure.

This colony of rare Australian fur seals seldom sees people. Dangerous Reef is a protected sanctuary, and visitors are allowed here by special permit only. Capkin and I separate and slowly move forward, careful not to startle the young animals. It is late morning, so most of the fur seal pups, already having eaten breakfast, are fast asleep on the warm rocks. Almost losing my balance on a slick boulder, I accidently dislodge a stone that bounces noisily down a ledge awakening a threesome of sleeping pups. I hastily sit down so my height and my standing on two legs doesn't

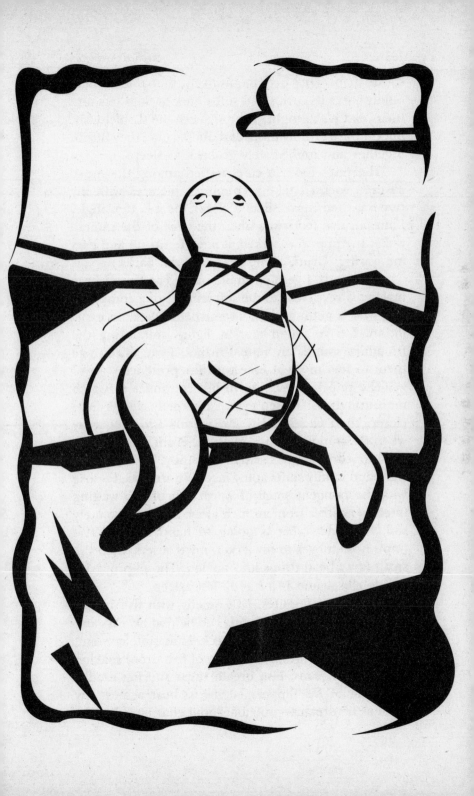

startle them. They peer inquisitively, then one of them boldly barks its curiosity. I softly bark back to reassure them that it's all right. The pups eye me suspiciously, but they are awfully tired, and one by one, they nuzzle together and immediately go back to sleep.

The pups look so cute nestled among the moss-covered rocks. I take a couple of pictures with my camera, then move silently closer for a better angle. I am but five feet away when the click of the camera wakes the pup who barked at me. He sits up and eyes me warily. "Gruff," (who are you?), he barks.

(A friend), I gently rumble back. The sound I am making is very close to the soft rumble of a contented dog who is getting its ears scratched. Often on expedition, I have found that by lightly mimicking the friendlier sounds an animal makes, I can encourage them to feel more at ease with my presence.

The pup lays back down but continues to watch me through half-closed eyes. I discreetly slide a little closer, then closer yet. I am merely two feet away when the pup warily sits up again. From close up, his eyes appear slightly crossed. Abruptly, he leans forward and loudly sniffs at my face. We are nose-to-nose with the pungent smell of warm fish breath wafting into my nostrils from an inch away. Sitting absolutely still, I wonder what is going to happen next. The pup's nose moves to my jacket, my trousers, then the small furry head drops into my lap. The pup nuzzles a little closer and is instantly fast asleep.

For fifteen minutes, I sit quietly with fish breath drooling on my jeans. I lightly rub behind his ears and stroke the soft fur under his neck. I am quite content, except for the warm, wet feeling of fish drool soaking into my 501 jeans. Fish breath starts snoring loudly, then one of his flippers begins to beat against my chest as he dreams—probably about chasing fish. Idly,

I glance about, then suddenly see Capkin waving urgently at me. He points anxiously towards another seal pup down closer to the water. It appears to be wrestling with itself as it rolls and thrashes in the sand. Then, I see the fishing net!

Quickly, I move the sleeping fur seal off my lap and scamper rapidly across the rocks. Capkin and I instantly agree on a soundless plan as both of us move in from opposite directions. The hapless fur seal is wearing a deadly necklace. Most of the nylon fishing net has been chewed away, except for a tight collar that encompasses the pup's neck. If the fishing net is not removed, the fur seal pup will suffer a terrible death by choking or suffocation.

The pup sees us coming and instantly flees towards the water. There is no opportunity for a slow or careful approach. If the pup reaches the surf, we won't be able to help it. Capkin and I rush forward. Leaping over a boulder, I am barely able to block its path to the water. The pup turns and starts to flee to my right, but Capkin does a diving tackle, capturing it at the last possible instant. Angry teeth attempt to bite, so we quickly wrap Capkin's jacket around its head. Unable to see, the young animal slowly becomes more manageable.

Talking softly to the frightened pup, I begin to examine the damage, which is horrible. The pup, which is about half a year old, has been wearing this deadly collar for several months. In that time the pup has grown, which means the unyielding nylon has bitten deeply into the soft skin around his throat. Using the scissors on my Swiss army knife, I begin cutting away the nylon strands. Some of them are buried a full quarter-inch deep into the tender flesh. The fur seal pup whimpers in pain, which breaks my heart. I whisper encouragement in soft words but continue to cut and gently pull away the deadly man-made fiber.

Finally, I am done. I take a few moments to examine the wound. There is very little swelling and no visible infection. I have no doubt that the pup will fully recover. I pet him lightly and tell him how brave he has been, then nod at Capkin to remove his jacket. Releasing the pup, we watch him run for the water. He plunges into an oncoming wave, then surfaces to peer back at us. He barks several times, not in gratitude, nor in anger; just a warning bark to other fur seals that dangerous humans are about.

Watching the small animal work its way out through the surf, I think how unlucky his short life has been so far. For us, just like the fur seal pup, life is a gamble. We never know what tragedies might overtake us. If life wasn't risky, it would not be so exciting. In every single day, there is a mystery waiting to be discovered. No one but God knows what rewards or penalties the future may hold. Life isn't particularly meant to be fair; things happen. Sometimes, it is no one's fault. So, if something should ever go terribly wrong in my life, I hope that the Lord will grant me the courage to accept what I cannot change. Meanwhile, I face life with a keen sense of humor, which I express often. Laughter is the best sort of medicine, though at the moment I am able to contain it as Capkin stares gloomily at a fur seal-chewed hole in his jacket.

Picking up the remains of the net, I signal the Zodiac to come get us. Then, looking back towards the rocks, I see the three sleeping pups and think about their future. Because of man, the South Australian fur seal is an endangered species: first because humans hunted them to near extinction for their fur pelts; now we compete with them for fish and sometimes catch the unwary seals in our nets.

People will probably never abandon net fishing, yet there are alternatives to what we are doing today. As with most businesses, money and profit are the prime motivators. Nylon nets do not biodegrade; when they break away and are lost at sea, the nylon nets continue to catch marine life. The net that caught this seal pup is encrusted with barnacles, which means it has been adrift for some time. Making fishing nets out of biodegradable materials means fish would cost a little more, but we would save a vast number of innocent marine creatures. Fishermen can be encouraged to use biodegradable nets if enough of us tell them how important it is to us. It just depends on how much we care.

There is also something constructive we can do at home to help wild animals. Soda cans sold by the six pack are often connected with a web of plastic. Each of the plastic loops is a potential noose for a bird or, if thrown into the water, for a fish. Tens of thousands of wild animals die horrible deaths because of these deadly plastic traps—that no one much thinks about. Next time you throw away these lethal plastic wraps, take a moment to cut the loops. Even better, consider recycling the plastic instead of throwing away a renewable resource.

Back on the *Alcyone*, the rest of the crew are sitting down to dinner. Capkin and I eagerly join the table of boisterous men. Most of the divers are taking large portions of the main course, which is fresh tuna. The man next to me raises a morsel of fish towards his mouth; abruptly his nose wrinkles as the fork stops in mid-air. "The fish stinks," he loudly announces.

The engineer, who caught the tuna with a fishing pole, is totally offended. "I just caught it this morning," he argues. "The fish is fine."

"I too smell decayed fish," states Antoine.

"It's Steve's pants," Capkin volunteers with a smile. "His jeans are soaked with fur seal drool."

After changing my pants, I return and take a helping of mashed potatoes and a large portion of green salad. I'm sure my fur seal pup friend would approve of my being a vegetarian. My decision leaves more fish for him.

> *Until he extends his circle of compassion to all living things, man will not himself find peace.* (Albert Schwitzer)

Twenty

You are my friends if you do what I command. I no longer call you servants, because a servant does not know his master's business. Instead, I have called you friends, for everything that I learned from my Father I have made known to you.

—John 15:14–15

The morning sun washes *Alcyone* with bright light as she races at full speed along the shoreline of Flores Island in Indonesia. It is a festive day, all of the windship's colorful signal flags fly from the turbo sails. Racing directly at us from the opposite direction is one of the most famous ships in the world. It is the *Calypso*.

This Indonesian rendezvous of the two Cousteau research vessels is tremendously exciting for the crews. For some, it is the opportunity to see old friends; for newer crew members like myself, it is the chance to make new ones.

Side-by-side the two ships sail into Flores harbor. *Calypso* drops anchor, then *Alcyone* ties up to her port side. A gang plank is run out to connect the two vessels, but some of *Calypso's* crewmen can't wait as they leap across to the deck of the windship. It is a merry time for all and an opportunity for me to explore Captain Cousteau's famous ship.

On *Calypso's* bridge, I can't resist spinning the giant brass wheel that is the ship's helm. Falco joins me there and, to his vast amusement, discovers that I speak very little French and that my accent is really horrible. Apparently, this earns me the honor of joining him at the lunch table.

A little before sunset, I launch a Zodiac and head toward the shoreline. There is an Indonesian village there built entirely on stilts over the water. The village is crowded with hundreds of wooden huts connected with narrow rickety walkways. Each of the tiny houses stands four to eight feet above the water. Beneath the huts lies an assortment of gaily colored canoes. Many of them have handpainted eyes to ward off evil spirits.

I enter the village through a small waterway. Passing under one of the narrow walkways, a group of children arrives at a run to inspect my strange canoe. They have never seen a boat that is mostly made of rubber and air. Several more children, in a yellow canoe with bird's eyes painted on the bow, paddle out and keep pace with the Zodiac. As more and more people arrive, and other canoes fall in the Zodiac's wake, my curious journey soon becomes a parade.

One of the boys leaps from a walkway onto the Zodiac's inflatable hull and bounces into the water. Instantly, a game is born as I am bombarded with laughing children. Most of them wind up in the water, but a few bounce and slide into the boat. When I reach the other end of the village, the Zodiac is crowded. There are more kids than I can count, plus two dogs, several lizards, a monkey, and a noisy parrot.

Unloading all the stowaways, I begin to motor slowly away, but the kids are yelling for me to make the canoe go fast. Opening up the throttle, the Zodiac leaps forward. At full throttle, the empty inflatable skims across the smooth water. At the tip of the village, silhouetted by the red orb of the setting sun, I see two children holding hands at the end of a pier. It is a boy and a girl. With joyous shrieks they leap into the water together. They wave from the water as I motor past.

On the distant horizon, I see *Calypso* and *Alcyone* laying alongside each other. I think about our rendezvous today and what made the event so special. It was the reunion of old friends and the sparkle of friendships about to be made.

Our happiness in life is dependent upon the quality of our relationships with others. It is friends that make ordinary events special—like the two kids laughing as they jumped into the water together. Surfing alone, without Antoine and Capkin, would quickly become boring. Sharing our worst fears with friends puts those fears into perspective, making them more tolerable. Friends add vitality, warmth, and unending excitement to life. There would be no thrill to adventure without a friend to share it with.

That night, as I lay myself down to sleep, I pause to stare at a picture taped to the side of my bunk. I see Cindy in a bridal gown, while I beam at the camera in my beard and tuxedo. Jean-Michel, our bestman, stands at my side. Crowded around us are the rest of the members of our wedding party. I think how lucky I am to have such wonderful friends and realize that now I am one of two; that together, Cindy and I are the beginning of a new family. It gives me great pleasure knowing that I no longer face life alone.

Two are better than one, because they have a good return for their work: If one falls down, his friend can help him up. (Eccles. 4:9–10)

Twenty-One

By Cindy Arrington

Your attitude determines your altitude.
                                        —Unknown

Taking a last deep breath of air, I dive beneath the water with eager anticipation. Though I am only in a swimming pool, the stakes are quite high. The Cousteau Society is going to hire three women divers for an upcoming expedition, and I desperately want to be one of them. Jean-Michel Cousteau intends to film the women divers swimming with a friendly pod of Atlantic spotted dolphins in the Bahamas. The key requirement is that the women divers must be able to swim rapidly, yet gracefully, and be able to hold their breath for two minutes or more.

At my side swims Margie Spielman, a marine artist from California and a fellow candidate. Together we go through a series of underwater maneuvers. Our movements blend together as we attempt an underwater ballet meant to mimic the social behavior of dolphins. To one side of the pool, I see sunlight glittering off Jean-Michel's face mask as he observes us. I can't help wondering if he knows how nervous I am. Finally, our lungs laboring for air, Margie and I shoot to the surface and eagerly swim over to Jean-Michel.

My heart is pounding as he calmly smiles and says "I'll have your airline tickets sent over tomorrow."

Two weeks later, we are in a Florida marina loading our equipment on a fifty-five-foot dive boat appropriately called *Dream Two*. In the late afternoon, we sail from the harbor with the outgoing tide. As the *Dream Two* slips out into the open ocean, Margie and I are at the plunging bow eagerly getting to know Beth Kneeland, the third member of our team. None of us can believe that we are on a voyage that will bring us underwater adventures we thought only existed in our dreams.

The following morning, we are up at first light. Eagerly, we survey the lightly rolling sea for dolphins. Under the tropical sun, it soon becomes hot and sultry. A light breeze generated by the forward motion of the boat provides little relief. I stare longingly at the cool water rushing pass the bow, then my heart leaps as I see a sleek gray shape racing just beneath the surface.

"Dolphins!" Margie shouts at my side. The sleek mammal surges out of the water as it races the bow wave. Another dolphin rises for a breath of air, then they are all about the boat—a dozen of them or more. The captain cuts the engines as everyone runs for their dive gear.

I barely have my mask and fins out of the dive bag when Jean-Michel abruptly shouts, "The dolphins are leaving. Somebody get in the water fast!"

Without thinking, I leap the railing and instantly hear twin shouts to my left and right. All three of us women hit the water together. There are bubbles everywhere from our entry; then through a shimmering curtain of rising bubbles, I see the dolphins returning. I begin mimicking their undulating style of swimming; instantly ten dolphins join me. Only inches separate us. I want to swim forever, but already my lungs are screaming for air. Looking toward the surface, all I can see are the white under bellies of dolphins. For a heart-pounding moment, I wonder if they might inadvertently prevent me from reaching the surface, yet as one we rise together. Inhaling deeply, I again descend with my flippered friends.

Below me, I see Margie diving straight down in a twisting spiral with a large dolphin in close attendance as though they are performing an underwater dance. A beam of sunlight paints the wonder of the moment forever in my memory. For two glorious hours, we swim and play with the dolphins while the cinematographer records our adventure on film.

After the dolphins depart, I lay on the deck basking in the sun as I let my mind drift, reliving the events of the day. I think how lucky I am to be here. Reflecting on my life, it pleases me that I've always sought adventure and self-improvement. When I was young, instead of idly watching television, my friends and I challenged each other to fun outside activities that helped develop our physical skills. Childhood accomplishments, like progressive stepping stones, paved the way toward bigger adventures. I have since realized that life is a never-ending challenge of potential quests that require the first step—after that, the lure of adventure takes care of the rest of the journey.

Abruptly, the crackle of static on the *Dream Two's* radio pulls at my attention. An announcer is counting down, "Three, two, one." I leap to my feet as another adventure is about to unfold in the sky above us. In the distance, I see a tiny speck that is the space shuttle *Discovery* rapidly climbing the horizon on a long tongue of fire. As I watch it streak across the sky, then disappear into the heavens, I think about the men and women inside the spaceship. With gratitude, I realize that I am of a generation where men and women work together as equals exploring our world from the vastness of space to the depths of the ocean.

Children at play are practicing living out their dreams on a daily basis. If we remain young inside, and remember to take time out to play, then our dreams can become our daily reality, too.

Twenty-Two

There is nothing like a dream to create the future.
—Victor Hugo

Running in the winter morning twilight, I leap a mossy rock, then bound across a half-frozen brook. The water babbles softly in the quiet of the frost-shrouded forest. An owl hoots from an old tree as I practice Indian running, eyes following the contours of the trail ahead while relying on my feet to sense the terrain they are crossing. The trick is to be light-footed, to just allow the soles to touch the ground before leaping forward.

It is a joy to run through the woods in the pale lunar light. I catch glimpses of the full moon between the tall pines and redwoods. Overhead, a squirrel scrambles across a branch creating a tiny cascade of falling snow crystals.

Several minutes later, the tree canopy begins to thin as the trail opens onto Sunset Lake. The broad shoreline wears a sparkling mantle of ice, and on the still water a Mallard duck paddles slowly with moonlight dancing in its wake.

Following the trail around the lake, I cross onto a dirt road. It is so wonderfully silent here in the mountains. I listen to the crunching sound of my feet on the frost, then abruptly hear a rumbling roar rushing through the woods. Twin orbs of blinding light career around a corner, then a huge logging truck hurls by just feet away. Trailing in its wake, a cloud of dust and debris flies stinging into my face. Digging grit from my eyes, I stare after the offending truck.

In less than five minutes, I dodge another speeding truck with its cargo of lifeless trees, then run onto a small rise where the forest unexpectedly ends. As far as I can see the land is empty of trees but for isolated patches here and there. Jogging reluctantly onward, I pass an endless chain of descending logging trucks—thirteen in an hour.

It is difficult for me to realize that the devastation of the forest is a willful act. Human greed consumes yet is never satisfied. It is a destroyer that devours forests and eats away at people's souls.

Staring at the ruined landscape, I realize that the forest and its animals are defenseless against greed, which is exactly why the Lord tasks us with caring for all the living things of the earth, great and small.

Obviously, we have to harvest lumber to build our homes and to make furniture, but we can do it without destroying the whole forest, through selective logging. In some areas, it is productive to create tree farms. We can also reduce the need for tree pulp if we care enough to recycle paper products. And, some people are doing much more.

Retracing my path back down the mountain, I soon see the tiny forest where my run began. Nestled among its trees is a Christian youth camp. Initially, it was a single person who first thought to save this tiny grove. It soon became a project that involved a whole church congregation. Through donations and hard work, many families spent years laboring together to buy, then care for this isolated patch of forest. From their endeavors, a legacy is born that will pass as a living inheritance to their children and to their children's children. These woods are a testimony that one dedicated person can always make a difference, particularly when his or her dreams are shared with family and friends.

Gratefully reentering the forest, I inhale the woodsy fragrance of the towering trees. At the babbling brook, I startle a doe and her fawn drinking; for a moment they stare with large innocent eyes, then bound into the woods.

At the trail's end, a warm yellow glow between two giant redwood trees reveals a cabin door opening; children's laughter lures me inside.

A dedicated person is capable of extraordinary feats, but a group of people working together can accomplish wonders.

Twenty-Three

Wisdom is a shelter as money is a shelter, but the advantage of knowledge is this: that wisdom preserves the life of its possessor.

—Ecclesiastes 7:12

Alcyone cuts rapidly through the swirling onrush of water. We are in Prince William Sound, traversing one of its narrower waterways. Here in the Northwestern Territories of Australia, the tidal flows are incredibly swift. The water can rise or fall up to thirty-three feet in six hours. The resulting tidal currents are so swift, particularly in these restricted channels, they create massive whirlpools. We are passing one just off to our starboard side. The whirlpool is at least fifty feet across with a swirling funnel that is fully five feet deep.

I stare nervously at the swirling vortex of water because one of our Zodiacs is headed right for it. Surprisingly, this is no accident. Two of our divers, Marc and Therry, are taking turns blasting through the edges of the whirlpools with the Zodiacs racing at full speed. They are both young men and find adventure in taking measured risks. I would prefer that they didn't go quite so close to the dangerous swirling water. Despite the daily risks we take on these expeditions, I am often referred to as the overprotective mother hen. I worry for the safety of my divers, and right now Therry is giving me something very real to worry about. At 30 MPH, he drops into the center of a massive whirlpool. For a heart-stopping moment, the small inflatable all but disappears from sight, then nose high it shoots nearly vertical out of the swirling pocket and goes bouncing out into smoother water.

Apparently, that daring move has ended their game. Therry and Marc return to the stern of the windship. Recovering the returning Zodiacs while *Alcyone* is racing at full speed is always an interesting and challenging feat. On the portside stern of the windship there is a ramp that goes down to the water. Antoine, Capkin, and I stand at the sides of the ramp ready to catch the first incoming Zodiac. It is an interesting experience to see an inflatable boat hurling at you, knowing your job is to try to catch it.

Marc makes the first run. The windship is racing at 15 MPH against a current flowing at 6 MPH, and Marc is charging the stern at about 25 MPH. The Zodiac hits the ramp hard, sliding forward fifteen feet as we pounce on it. Removing the outboard engine and lifting out the fuel tank takes less than a minute. Then, we prepare to receive the second Zodiac. This maneuver is much more tricky. Our ramp is short and narrow, so we must stack the inflatable boats one on top of the other. Marc has landed the smaller of the two Zodiacs, which the four of us now lift up and hold on our shoulders. Therry's job is to make a high-speed deposit of his larger Zodiac underneath the smaller one we are lifting. Considering that the Zodiac we are holding up weighs over two hundred pounds, it is important that Therry land his boat quickly.

Antoine offers a bit of encouragement, "Hurry up, my grandmother could park it faster than you."

With the first boat balanced on our shoulders, I see Therry grinning wickedly as he hurls at us with the throttle almost wide open. An instant later, the bow hits the ramp, bounces up, and slams all the way to the back of the ramp. I look down at the Zodiac abruptly resting at my feet. There is less than a two-inch gap between my legs and the inflatable boat. We quickly secure both Zodiacs.

Sometimes, we leave one of the Zodiacs tied to the stern; however, we are about to go up the Prince Regent River. The Captain did not think it would be a good idea to leave a rubber boat in the water since this river is a home for saltwater crocodiles.

I quickly hustle to the bow as we head for the river mouth. I am about to see an amazing sight. The tidal outflow is at its peak, which means the water level is falling about eight feet an hour. To our port side closer to shore, there is an exposed reef with a broad tidal waterfall flowing vigorously down its sides. The reef has a flat table-like top, and the sea water is cascading down multiple levels back to the sea. An ocean waterfall is something I never expected to see.

As *Alcyone* begins her journey up the river, the water turns a muddy brown. Anxiously, I watch the shore, eager for my first sight of a salt-water crocodile. Unfortunately, over the next two hours I don't see a single crocodile. Not that they are not about, it is just that they hear the windship's engines coming and have learned to duck out of sight. I pause to wipe the sweat off my face. Australian summers get really hot; it is 114 degrees Fahrenheit in the shade, so I go below deck to the dive locker to cool off and get some work done.

Late in the afternoon, the whole crew is on deck as we round a final bend in the river and arrive at King's Cascade. We find a safe place to anchor, not far from a crudely painted sign on the rocks that forbids swimming because of the crocodiles.

"No kidding," I think to myself.

Nicholas, *Alcyone's* captain, paces the deck. He is not comfortable anchoring for the night in this tiny inlet. Even though our government guide assures us the tidal change will not be any greater than ten feet this far up the river, the captain decides to take some precautions. He has Therry and Marc attach mooring lines to the rocky cliffs and around a tree on the shore. This is to ensure the windship's safety and to keep us over a flat mud bottom just in case the government man is wrong about the amount of tidal change this far up river.

We no sooner finish when I see my first crocodile. Actually, there are two of them lying on a distant rock. For a moment, I pause to think of the young American film actress who lost her life here. As the day begins to fade towards twilight, I am distracted from my thoughts by the sound of the chef ringing the dinner bell. Capkin, of course, beats me below deck.

At the dinner table, most of the conversation centers around salt-water crocodiles. Our guide explains that they are the largest reptiles in the world and can grow to lengths of eighteen feet or more. Because of overhunting, they became an endangered species here, but now that they're protected, they are making a rapid recovery. The guide is just explaining how they work together to rip apart their prey when the saloon lights abruptly fade and the ship goes dark.

"If this is a joke, it's not funny," Capkin states in a flat voice around a mouthful of food.

Two crewmen race into the engine room while the rest of us surge up onto the deck. We are astonished to discover that the water in the little bay is almost completely gone, but for a puddle under the waterfall. The windship has settled onto the mud bottom. The soft mud is so deep the *Alcyone* is still perfectly level. A moment later one of the engineers arrives to report that the ship's generators shut down because of a lack of cooling water.

The captain looks at our government guide and shakes his head. The outgoing tide dropped the water level here a full twenty-eight feet. "Looks like we are stuck here for at least the next six hours—without lights or power." The captain is far from happy.

Capkin plays a flashlight beam along the shore-line. Numerous pairs of close-set reptilian eyes reflect the light in a hellish red glow. "I guess they're making a comeback," declares Capkin. "Look at all those buggers."

The guide is looking at the deck in shame as he says, "You should know that crocodiles have been known to climb onto boat decks, particularly late at night."

"Well, that's a cheery thought," I reply.

Therry reaches over and closes the access gate to the stern. "I don't think I'll be sleeping on deck to-night," he states wistfully, "and it is going to be really hot below without air conditioning."

"Well, since we're not going anywhere," Capkin says, heading back below, "think I'll go finish my din-ner."

Most of us have trouble sleeping that night in the sweltering heat, so we gather in the saloon and under the soft glow of candle light share the scariest stories we know. Occasionally, we would hear a loud thump of something banging against the outside hull, but none of us volunteered to go outside to see what it was.

Twenty-Four

The way of a fool seems right to him, but a wise man listens to advice. A fool shows his annoyance at once, but a prudent man overlooks an insult.

—Proverbs 12:15–16

At three in the morning, the water returns, refloating *Alcyone*. To everyone's relief, we start the generators and get the air conditioning going. Since it is dangerous to navigate an unknown river at night, we decide to wait for the morning light before getting underway.

At six o'clock in the morning, after only two hours of restless sleep, I am not in the best of moods. We put a Zodiac in the water so the government guide and I can go ashore to untie two of the mooring lines. The guide has kept a low profile throughout the night and is now eager to be of assistance after helping to cause last night's disastrous situation. In fact, he is being a little too helpful. I'm standing on the shore trying to untie a muddy knot from around a tree, and he is in the boat offering unneeded advice.

"It's not a good idea standing there, mate," he cautions.

"How else am I going to untie the knot?" I know I'm being discourteous, but the last thing I want is advice from him.

"Well, if you get back in the boat, we could drag ourselves closer by pulling in on the mooring line," he says hopefully.

Actually, it is a pretty good idea, not that I am in a frame of mind to admit it. "I'm almost done, besides if a croc shows up I'll see him coming."

"No you won't," he says looking around fearfully. "They can attack without warning."

The guide is really getting to me. Angrily, I jerk and pull at the jammed knot, while glancing nervously towards the water's edge. Despite his warnings, I am convinced that in order to see me a crocodile would have to show himself before attacking. By keeping a wary eye on the water, I don't doubt I will see the croc coming.

Finally, the knot comes apart, and I thankfully step back into the Zodiac. I am quite pleased to prove to the guide that it really was not a big deal. He shrugs and holds onto the mooring line so the guys at the stern of the windship can pull us back. Soon, we are underway and thankfully heading back down the river.

Two weeks later, we are in Broome, a coastal town south of Prince Regent Sound. We are spending the weekend taking on stores, so I decide to go on an excursion. There is a crocodile farm here, and I decide to visit it. Considering that I am doing research for The Cousteau Society, the manager is quite pleased to take me on a behind-the-scenes tour. Notebook in hand, I ask a few questions and dutifully write down his replies. Without really thinking about it, I tell him about my argument with the guide and my comment that a crocodile has to see you before attacking.

"Tell you what mate," comes his cheerful reply. "Go grab that bucket over there, and I'll show you something."

The bucket in question is laying beside a chain-link fence. On the other side of the fence is an apparently empty crocodile pen with a pool of muddy water. As I'm bending over to pick up the bucket, my eyes happen to be on the perfectly still surface of the pool. Then, without any warning, a huge crocodile erupts from the muddy water and crashes into the chain link right at the level of my head. The fence bulges grossly outward with massive teeth embedded in it. The crocodile's mouth is momentarily wedged wide open. Extremely bad reptile breath pants directly into my face as I stare in complete shock. For a frozen moment, my feet are locked in place, then I jump rapidly away.

The crocodile jerks its teeth free, then it furiously slams its tail repeatedly against the chain links. It glares at me and hisses loudly.

"No," laughs the manager over my shoulder, "offhand, I'd say they don't have to see you at all."

"You knew he was going to do that?" I'm not quite stuttering but am having trouble catching my breath.

"Yeah," the manager is very pleased with himself. "Old Jacques don't like anyone near his cage. He's pretty nasty even for a croc."

"Why didn't you at least warn me?" I ask.

"Look at it this way mate," he says, placing a hand on my shoulder. "You just learned something about crocodiles in a way that makes a lasting impression."

"I guess."

"Crocodiles can sense sound vibrations through the bottom of their lower jaw. So, they can pretty much tell the exact location of something on the beach or shore by their victim's foot steps." The manager reaches into the bucket and picks out a hunk of meat, which he casually flips over the fence. The meat barely hits the ground, when Jacques erupts from the water, snags the meat, and drags it back below the muddy surface.

"The guide was right, those crocs knew exactly where you were," he raises an eyebrow to emphasize his point. Then he says, "Don't you want to know why I named him Jacques?"

"After Jacques Cousteau?" I offer.

"Na, use to be the name of my dog," the man is staring somewhat longingly at the empty surface of the water. "The dog walked right down to the water to get a drink, and the croc got him."

"So, you still miss him?" I ask.

"Na," he dead pans, "the mutt wasn't very bright."

I leave the crocodile park a little bit wiser and not just about crocodiles. I realize how foolish I had been; because of my anger, I wouldn't listen to someone who knew more about a subject than I did. It could have cost me my life.

> *No discipline seems pleasant at the time, but painful. Later on, however, it produces a harvest of righteousness and peace for those who have been trained by it.* (Heb. 12:11)

Twenty-Five

The children of today are tyrants. They talk back to their elders, slobber their food, and annoy their teachers.
—Socrates

Walking down the gang plank, I am anxious to rejoin my friends on *Alcyone*. The windship has been idle here in Fiji for two months between expeditions. I know everyone is anxious to get back to work. Life is always more fun and full of challenge when people enjoy their jobs. It is a wise and fortunate person who chooses a career which offers pleasure as well as personal satisfaction.

It is just after sunrise, and no one is topside yet. I pause for a moment to revel in the anticipation of another expedition about to begin. I delight in the wonderful feeling of a light tropical breeze bearing the fragrance of fresh fruit and cooking smells wafting in from a seaside open market. People are walking the street in colorful sarongs as the seaport awakens to another day.

Stepping onto the windship, I industriously pound the deck with my feet. The racket brings Therry and Capkin hurrying up from below.

"It is Steve," Therry yells to the men below, "and he has presents."

The rest of the crew rushes to the deck to see what I have brought. Whenever I join *Alcyone*, I bring

132

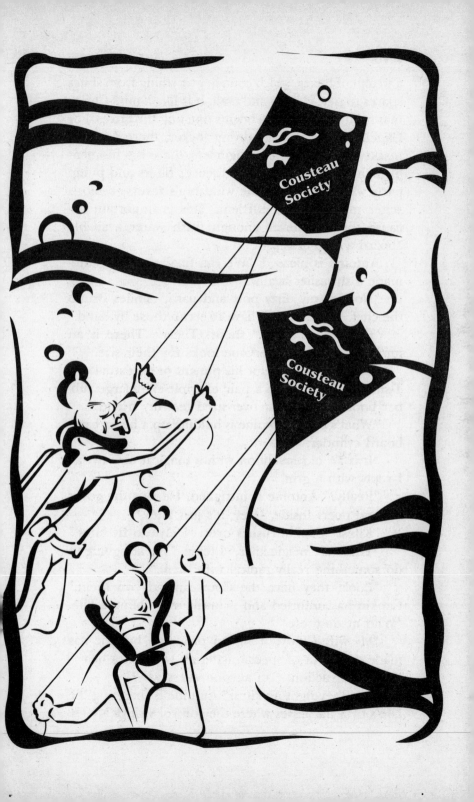

a wealth of boxes, which contain everything from ship's spares to new clothes and mail. It is like a mini-Christmas in July as everyone begins opening the boxes. For Capkin, who runs our diving locker, there are new masks and fins. For the engineers, there is a moment of high excitement as they discover filters and pump parts which will make the windship's reverse-osmosis water makers more efficient. This is important because there is never enough fresh water available aboard a ship at sea.

Antoine is pleased, "We can finally use the automatic dishwasher again."

"Not for my dirty pots and pans," smiles Bruno the chef. "You will still have to scrub those by hand."

"Cousteau T-shirts," shouts Therry. There is an immediate rush as everyone looks for their size.

"Capkin," I interrupt his pursuit of an extra-large T-shirt by holding up a pair of triple-extra-large rubber booties, "for your over-sized feet my friend."

"What's this?" Antoine is holding up a heavy cardboard cylinder.

"It is an old invention with a magical new twist," I reply with a grin.

"Really?" Antoine is intrigued. He rips the cover off and peers inside, "Hey, it's just kites."

"Kites!" Capkin rushes over. "I love to fly kites."

"These are magic kites," I tease. "We are going to do something really radical with them."

"Look, they have the Cousteau lady on them," Capkin has unfurled and is busily assembling a kite. "Who made these?"

"My wife Cindy," I answer proudly, "but she has made them out of special materials with extra heavy-duty construction. Can anyone guess why?"

"Are they fighting kites?" Antoine is fingering the kite's twin harnesses where the control strings attach.

"Yes, they are designed for aerobatics, however, we will be flying them underwater," I answer, eager for their reactions.

"Underwater?" Antoine is astonished.

"Cool," Capkin as always is totally enthusiastic, "this is a great idea."

I grin, acknowledging the compliment, "They are made with lightweight nylon, and the spars are extra strong for flexibility and added strain. The tails are short to reduce drag underwater."

"Kites can't fly underwater." Antoine is not convinced.

"Yes they can," I answer, "because water is more dense than air, a mile-per-hour underwater current is equal in force to a 30 MPH wind. The kites will fly underwater."

"Let's go try them." Capkin is ready to go.

"We can't," I reply. "Jean-Michel says we have to wait for him. He will be here tomorrow."

The following morning Jean-Michel arrives, and *Alcyone* gets underway for our next step on this round-the-world exploration of discovery. However, it is several days before we get the opportunity to test the kites. Our first few dives we spend working, capturing reef life on film, and testing a new set of underwater lights.

Finally, and barely soon enough for Capkin, we go on the kite dive. Actually, this will be a regular working dive, however, we are going very deep, over one hundred and sixty feet. This means we will end the dive with long decompression stops at thirty, twenty, and ten feet. Jean-Michel decides that we will test the kites during the long—and boring—decompression stops.

The deep dives are always exciting, and this one is exceptional. The reef we are diving on is a vertical wall. We descend quickly down its steep sides. The reef wall is alive with passionate colors of vibrant marine life that slowly fades in color as we go deeper and deeper to where the filtered sunlight barely reaches. About us, the reef turns shades of dark blue, deep green, and lifeless gray, but it is all an illusion caused by the lack of natural light.

My main job underwater when we are filming is to hold the movie lights. In my hands is a metal frame that contains sixteen brilliant projector bulbs. It is like carrying a miniature sun underwater. I play its intense beam across the reef, and wherever the light beam touches, the reef's magnificent colors spring to life. It is like painting with a ray of light.

A black tip reef shark swims into view. I splash forty-eight hundred watts of blazing light across its side, which causes the shy animal to flee in alarm. At one hundred and sixty-five feet, we encounter a huge school of barracuda. There are hundreds of them swimming close together like a living metallic curtain that my lightbeam washes over in a broad glistening reflective arch. The barracudas' scales glitter like diamonds as they bounce the light back into the twilight of deep water. Swimming into the vast school, the fish part before us like a pulsating silver wave that reforms as we pass. It is a beautiful dive that ends all too soon. My decompression meter indicates that it is time to leave. I wave the light to capture each divers' attention, then signal for all to ascend.

We swim up slowly, never faster than the smallest bubble from our last exhalation. It is to prevent our getting the dreaded bends, a diver's malady from ascending too fast. It is a long, slow ascent as I watch our bubbles bouncing in a long buoyant chain toward the surface. At thirty feet, we reach our first stop to begin our decompression. I signal the Zodiacs waiting above us with my light. The engineers quickly stop the generator that drives our lights, then pull them up into the inflatable boat. Anxiously, we watch the bottom of the Zodiac. Then, one of the engineers jumps into the water. With rapid strokes of his fins, he swims two kites down to eagerly waiting hands.

Despite the fact that flying kites underwater was my idea, Jean-Michel and Capkin wind up with the kites. We have selected an ideal site for the test. The divers are somewhat sheltered from a strong two knot current by the reef. Its jagged wall also allows them a place to anchor their feet, yet the kites will be exposed to the strong current. Surprisingly, Jean-Michel is first to launch his kite. Capkin, in his excitement, has managed to get tangled in the control lines.

Jean-Michel's kite takes to the water, just as Cindy designed. It climbs, twists, and turns just like a kite caught in the wind, but all of its movements are in slow motion, which adds elegance to the maneuvers. Jean-Michel flies it past a sea fan that is bent horizontally from the current, then he uses it to chase a coral trout that quickly seeks refuge in a crevice.

Capkin, finally untangling the string from his fins, mask, and scuba tank, launches a surprise attack on Jean-Michel's kite. As the two divers do battle with the fighter kites, passing fish stare in wonder, then flee in alarm. The extended underwater war carries us through the thirty and twenty foot decompression stops with no apparent winner. I am eagerly waiting to see what happens as Jean-Michel crowds Capkin's kite close to a giant clam, when Therry runs out of air.

First of all, this is not an entirely unusual circumstance. Therry has breathed his scuba cylinder dry, which means he needs to transfer over to one of the decompression cylinders dangling beneath the Zodiac. Only Therry, caught up in the excitement of the kite war, is too far from the safety cylinders. He begins to swim frantically in their direction, but I have heard the distinctive hollow ring that a scuba regulator makes when the air pressure is low. Instantly, I swim to Therry's side offering him air from my regulator. The standby tanks are not far away, and together we make the short swim buddy-breathing.

Five minutes later, Jean-Michel gets the advantage when Capkin is distracted by an eel peering at him from a hole in the reef. The experiment, and our decompression over, the team swims to the surface and climbs into the waiting Zodiacs.

"I won," pronounces Jean-Michel, thus concluding the first ever underwater kite war.

"Excuse me Jean-Michel," I ask, "didn't you notice that we had an out-of-air-situation?"

"But, of course," answers Jean-Michel, "and I knew you would handle it very well. I, however, was involved in intense underwater warfare."

"And, you won," offers Capkin.

"So, what's your point?" Jean-Michel asks me, as he admires his kite.

"Well, I thought I might get to fly one of the kites," I offer lamely.

"And you shall," smiles Jean-Michel, "however, this is my kite. Maybe Capkin will loan you his."

The kites were, of course, a big hit. Often at anchorage, we would fly them off the stern of the windship. When Jean-Michel told his father about the kites, Jacques Cousteau asked Cindy to make several hundred more, which he took to Russia to give to the children. They made a festival out of it. The sky over a dismal industrial town on the Danube River abruptly came alive with a multitude of colorful kites and the sound of children laughing.

The afternoon after our kite dive, Capkin and I fly our kites in the tropical trade winds. We laugh together and wonder why some people labor at chores they don't enjoy. The world is full of opportunity for those who are willing to risk a challenge. Life is meant to be exciting, mysterious, and full of adventure. Why should anyone choose less than that? The only injustice in life is that I haven't gotten a chance at challenging Jean-Michel to an underwater kite duel.

> *Moreover, when God gives any man wealth and possessions, and enables him to enjoy them, to accept his lot and be happy in his work–this is a gift of God. He seldom reflects on the days of his life, because God keeps him occupied with gladness of heart.* (Eccles. 5:19–20)

Twenty-Six

If we did all the things we are capable of doing, we would literally astonish ourselves.

—Thomas Edison

Pulling on my rubber wetsuit, I am looking forward to another dive with Scarface—not that it is his real name. I don't think the big fish cares what I call him, he just wants to be friends—and maybe share some of my lunch. I have a half-pound block of cheese stuffed inside the front of my wetsuit. The smell, even underwater, will make me irresistible to the one-hundred-and-fifty-pound grouper.

"You better hope that the chef doesn't notice that someone is stealing his cheese," cautions Jean-Michel.

"Actually, he thinks Capkin has been raiding the refrigerator in the middle of the night," I answer with a grin.

"Why do I always have to be the one who gets blamed for missing food?" complains Capkin. He is holding a waterproof case that looks surprisingly like a lunch box.

"Taking down a snack?" asks Jean-Michel.

"It's just some leftovers for the fish," Capkin beams. Stepping to the edge of *Alcyone's* stern, he leaps into the water before anyone can ask him questions about missing food. Rapidly, the rest of the five-man dive team follows.

We are at Rowley Shoals, an isolated chain of reefs, several hundred miles from Australia's north-western shore. Beneath the windship, there is a rather unique underwater spot called Grouper Hole. It is a small piece of reef which is home to a dozen large groupers who don't seem to mind a little human companionship. Dive boats regularly bring tourists out to swim with the big fish, and we are here to document this special relationship.

Descending down into the clear cool water, it isn't long before the first of the big groupers arrives. Capkin doesn't notice its presence until he feels an abrupt tugging on his box. Turning in mid-water, he looks in surprise to find that one of the giant groupers has its big lips wrapped completely around his lunch box. Jerking back doesn't free the hostage box. Finally, he places a finned-foot against big lips' nose and pries the box free.

However, this does not end Capkin's problems. The fish is extremely eager to latch onto the lunch box again. Capkin tries hiding it behind his back, but other arriving groupers instantly target the tempting lunch box. Finally, Capkin wedges himself against the reef and carefully opens the box with the intent of offering a small handout. The open box is irresistible for the grouper gang as the big fish descend aggressively on Capkin.

Groupers do not bite as much as they inhale. They open their massive mouths a full foot or more, then, like giant vacuum cleaners, suck in their prey. In this case, the prey consists of leftover tuna from lunch and a peanut butter and jelly sandwich in plastic wrap that Capkin may have actually been saving for himself. In trying to save the sandwich, he only manages to rescue the empty plastic wrapper.

Having pillaged Capkin's lunch, it doesn't take the groupers long to figure out who is holding the cheese. I quickly break the block of cheese into smaller pieces, which I attempt to share one at a time. However, I soon realize that fish are not aware of the concept of sharing.

After pillaging me, the groupers quickly examine each member of the team to make sure no one else is holding any more goodies. Some of the big fish instantly lose interest in the now foodless divers and swim off, but half of them remain to play. Each of us divers soon has a fish friend. Capkin's fish buddy is a sleek teen-ager. They chase each other about the reef playing hide-and-seek. Meanwhile, I smile at scarface as he swims up for a little attention. He particularly likes for me to scratch around his gills. Scarface is a very ugly fish; fortunately he isn't aware of his horrendous looks. The big fish has a rather nasty scar on his forehead. It looks like he may have tried rubbing up against a spinning propeller. Well, fish are not known for being very bright. Speaking of which, I notice that Jean-Michel is getting more attention from a grouper than he may have planned for. His fish likes him so much it is demonstrating mating behavior. This consists mainly of color changes in its skin tones, but it also includes a rather odd ritual of bumping its belly against the top of Jean-Michel's head. The rest of us divers find this harmless behavior very amusing. Our only regret is our limited bottom time which causes us to depart our fish friends a half hour later.

After dinner, I go to the stern of the windship to watch the sunset and find Jean-Michel staring idly out to sea.

"What are you thinking about?" I ask.

"The groupers," Jean-Michel answers. "This spot is so unique. How many places in the world do you know of where humans and fish are friends and actually play together?"

"I don't know of any place," I reply. "Usually if a fish gets too close to a person, it winds up in a frying pan."

"Exactly," Jean-Michel sadly replies, "which is what worries me. Something wonderful and totally unique is happening here. Yet, one idiot with a spear gun could completely wipe out every one of these groupers in half an hour."

"How do we prevent that?" I ask candidly.

"My father once said that people protect what they love," Jean-Michel replies. "It's the answer. If enough people see our film and realize how important these fish really are, they may insist on this reef becoming a protected sanctuary."

An incoming radio call pulls Jean-Michel away. Standing at the stern, watching the fiery red globe of the sun descend into a quiet sea, I stare at the light dancing on the water and think about the groupers swimming quietly below. If the friendly residents of Grouper Hole can survive, these few fish can awaken in man a new appreciation of our own lives and for the incredible wonder of one of God's creations. To save these few fish would be a tiny investment, but the potential rewards for the spirit of mankind are astonishingly huge.

> *"Bring the whole tithe into the storehouse, that there may be food in my house. Test me in this," says the Lord Almighty, "and see if I will not throw open the floodgates of heaven and pour out so much blessing that you will not have room enough for it." (Mal. 3:10–12)*

Twenty-Seven

One man gives freely, yet gains even more; another withholds unduly, but comes to poverty. A generous man will prosper; he who refreshes others will himself be refreshed.

—Proverbs 11:24–25

Two tourist dive-boats arrive at Grouper Hole, so Jean-Michel decides we should weight anchor and head for less crowded waters. Scott Reef lies three hundred miles further to the north. We are hoping that the reef's remote location will make for ideal diving conditions. The more inaccessible reefs almost always have more abundant marine life. As *Alcyone* sails into the night, none of us could have anticipated what the morning would bring.

Scott Reef is a long chain of shallow shoals and jagged reefs with a tiny island toward its center. The little island barely stands eight feet above the ocean with almost no vegetation on its few acres of barren ground. As such, we are not anticipating to see much of anything above water—so the small fleet of Indonesian fishing vessels at anchor here comes as quite a surprise. There are over a dozen of the crudely built wooden boats. Each is about forty feet long with a crew of eight to ten men and boys.

While we maneuver *Alcyone* toward an anchorage, two of the Indonesian boats run up their sails and

head in our direction. As they approach, I notice that
their sails are made from common plastic tarps. It is
a sure indication that these fishermen are from a very
poor village. Desperation has driven them a long way
from their homes in Indonesia. With only cheap com-
passes as their guides, they have come over a thousand miles to fish these remote waters.

The two boats appear to be racing as they tack off
to our port side, where they quickly lower their sails.
The competing crews rush as they each launch a canoe, which the men and boys frantically begin paddling towards the stern of *Alcyone*. As the ship's medic,
I have immediate concerns that they may have a medi-
cal emergency. Yet, as the two crews arrive at the back
of the windship, their urgent need turns out to be
something much more basic.

"Water," shouts a twelve-year-old boy, "please." He
is holding up an empty five gallon water can. The
other canoe arrives with the same compelling request.

Reaching for the youth's empty container, I notice
that both canoes are full of empty water containers.
The men and boys in the canoes stare up hopefully.
Looking toward the other boats, I notice they are all
raising sails and heading in our direction.

"I think we are about to have a lot of company,"
I say to Jean-Michel.

"And just a limited amount of water," replies Jean-
Michel. *Alcyone's* reverse-osmosis water filters can con-
vert less than six hundred gallons of sea water into
drinking water a day. To fill the containers in just one
canoe would take a fourth of our total water supply,
and there are over a dozen boats headed in our direction. Yet, there is one additional component that makes
Jean-Michel's decision even more complicated.

The main limiting factor in the length of time the
fishing boats can stay on the reef is determined by the

amount of water they carry. The more water we give them, the longer the Indonesians can stay to pillage the reef. It is a horrible dilemma because these people are trying to support families back home. Yet, the fish and other marine life they are taking are not strictly for their personal consumption. The goal of the fishermen is to sell their catch so they will have money to buy consumable items like motor scooters and televisions.

Jean-Michel makes an instant decision. "Give only twenty gallons of water to each boat. Then, get the dive team together, I want to check the condition of this reef."

That afternoon, we dive an extraordinarily beautiful reef that is practically devoid of fish. The Indonesians come from an extremely over-populated country. Their reefs are mostly picked bare, which means they must range further and further to realize even a modest profit. These people are poor and living under adverse conditions; they cannot be blamed for wanting to take care of their families and raise their standard of living. But, does that mean we should contribute to the continued destruction of Scott Reef? It is a question without an easy answer.

Meanwhile, we are discovering something fascinating about the underwater world of Scott Reef. The place is crowded with sea snakes. Considering that the snakes are not very large does not decrease the respect these reptiles have earned. The sea snake is one of the most venomous animals in the world. Their bite is almost always fatal. Fortunately, their mouths are very small, which means they cannot bite through our wetsuits, nor our rubber gloves.

Despite our supposed protection, we are extremely careful around the marine reptiles. It turns out that Antoine has a very real fear of snakes. He keeps his distance from the slithering reptiles, but is completely unaware that one is behind him. It is only curious and soon swims away. Our dive causes some amusement among the Indonesian fishermen. Lacking fins and wearing goggles carved from wood and plastic, they are accompanying us on our dive of exploration. Noticing our preoccupation with the sea snakes, they decide to perform for us. The men and boys grab the deadly snakes barehanded and take them to the surface for play. They wrap them around their throats like neckties. Incredibly the sea snakes don't bite, which would be fatal. The Indonesians refer to them as their friends.

In a modern society, it is sometimes apparently easy to attempt to define the world in scientific terms, but our planet is too big and diverse for that. These unassuming people who call a deadly animal friend are simply being honest. Their culture has not taught them to fear sea snakes. They know the world from a different perspective than modern cultures. We shop for our food in stores; they shop by fishing, farming, and gathering. We fear sea snakes because we know them to be potentially fatal, yet the villagers, who have never been bitten, know them as friends.

When people in a modern society fear a creature, their normal response is to kill it. In America, when someone kills a shark, there is almost never any sympathy for the shark. The word *shark* is one of the most feared words in our language. When we swim in the ocean, almost all Americans fear the possibility of a shark attack. Yet, this is such a rare occurrence that we stand a much better chance of being struck by a lightning bolt.

As we continue our dive, Jean-Michel leads us deeper down the side of the reef, and, abruptly, there is an explosion of marine life. The Indonesian fishermen with their crude goggles are limited to the first twenty feet of water depth. They have not yet learned to reach these depths, but one day they will. There is no simple solution to this and other global problems. Yet, the way we approach these worldwide problems does have a simple answer.

> For this very reason, make every effort to add to your faith goodness; and to goodness, knowledge; and to knowledge, self-control; and to self-control, perseverance; and to perseverance, godliness; and to godliness, brotherly kindness; and to brotherly kindness, love. (2 Pet. 1:5–7)

Back on the *Alcyone*, we share the water that we have, and, to make more water available to the fishermen, we forsake our daily showers. The grateful fishermen tell us that our arrival has saved them from having to go to the island's well where the water is bad. Earlier in the afternoon, we had gone to the island. The well the fisherman is referring to has signs around it that say "Danger, Cholera!" If they drank there, some of the Indonesians would die. For them, it is a fact of the harshness of their lives.

Toward sunset, I am standing at the back of the windship when a couple of the Indonesian boys swim to our stern to beg for a drink. Getting a pitcher of refrigerated water, I forget to bring glasses. So, the boys place their hands together to drink from them like a cup. They are surprised by the chill of the water, but not so foolish as to separate their hands and let the precious water flow out. While pouring the water, I think how two hands placed together is a sign for friendship and for sharing. It reflects a state of mind where people can work together, whereas a single hand raised as a fist in anger means there will never be any easy solutions. Our best chance for solving the vast problems of the world is to approach them together.

When the water is gone, the boys prepare to return to their boats. Urging them to wait, I rush below to get several of our kites and bring them out onto the deck. The kids are thrilled. In Indonesia, making kites is a national pastime. We fly the kites together well into the twilight. When the boys leave, laughing as they swim off into the night, I determine that tomorrow Capkin and I will fly our kites for them underwater. That should give them an interesting story to take back to their village.

Twenty-Eight

Know that there is nothing better for men than to be happy and do good while they live. That everyone may eat and drink, and find satisfaction in all his toil–this is the gift of God.

—Ecclesiastes 3:12–13

Old Charlie is a rather strange name for a bottle-nose dolphin. Yet, Old Charlie wasn't exactly your typical dolphin. He liked to hang out in a quiet little inlet called Monkey Mia in Shark Bay, part of the remote Northwestern Territories of Australia. The year was 1956, and Old Charlie had a fisherman friend who would occasionally toss the dolphin a fish or two. Not too many people knew very much about dolphins back then, but that was about to change in a very big way.

The fisherman was just leaving the pier in his boat when he spied a school of anchovies inside the harbor. He quickly maneuvered to set his net, but, at the last moment, the school of fish escaped the closing net. Yet, before he could pull in the empty net, Old Charlie rushed into the harbor and chased the entire school of fish back into the mouth of the net. The fisherman was ecstatic with his catch.

From that day forward, Old Charlie occasionally helped the man catch fish, and, in return, he got all the fish he could eat. Dolphins being social creatures,

Old Charlie began bringing a few friends by, and pretty soon there was a whole pod of dolphins hanging out at Monkey Mia. This astounded the local people, who would flock to a nearby beach to feed the amiable dolphins. Sometimes, special human/dolphin friendships would result. A sure indication that a dolphin liked a person was when it started bringing him or her fish.

Twenty-three years later, Monkey Mia is now world famous for its large pod of friendly dolphins, and I couldn't wait to see them. At sunrise, *Alcyone* sails into the quiet inlet with the morning tide and drops anchor a few hundred yards offshore. Capkin, Antoine, and I quickly launch a Zodiac and motor into the beach. Along the way we pick up two dolphin hitchhikers who trail the inflatable into the beach. Capkin, unable to contain his excitement, can't resist leaping into the water with them. Soon, he is cavorting about, mimicking the unique swimming style of the dolphins, but only at about one-tenth their speed.

Antoine and I drag the Zodiac up onto the beach, then head in the general direction of a large crowd. About two hundred people are standing knee-deep in the water, while various dolphins swim up and down the beach collecting friendly pets and an occasional fresh fish handout. A ranger is present to ensure that the crowd of people stays in the shallow water so as not to alarm or endanger the dolphins.

At the edge of the beach, there is a truck where people are buying fish to feed to the dolphins. One of the children in line looks rather odd; then I realize that I am looking at a four-foot tall pelican. The bird, named Wally, is quite bold in his pursuit of fish. He has been known to ambush small children attempting to carry fish to the dolphins.

Stepping out into the water, I spend the next

couple of hours photographing this unique human/
dolphin relationship. In the late afternoon, I'm standing in chest-deep water when a mother dolphin arrives with her two-month-old calf. The hungry mother
eagerly swims straight into the beach in search of a
fish handout or two. The calf, however, is too shy to
brave all the people. She swims nervously back and
forth thirty yards from the shore. Lowering my head
beneath the surface, I hear the calf calling nervously
to its mother. Underwater, the high-pitched squeaks
have a haunting sound that I can't resist answering.

Instantly, the calf hones in on my call and begins
to curiously circle me. The calf, only about three feet
long, is swimming sideways so she can peer up at me.
I continue to squeak and chirp while standing in place
so as not to startle her. Soon, mom has a bellyful of
free fish and swims over to check me out. Apparently,
I'm OK, because she rubs once against my bare leg,
then calling to her baby, leads the calf back out to sea.

That night, I fell asleep and dreamed that I was
swimming in the open ocean with Bent Fin. (The
ranger on the beach told me the calf's name.)

The next morning, I am the first one out on the
stern of the windship. Sitting on the deck, I sip a cup
of hot chocolate while watching the sunrise. It is so
quiet and pleasant with a light trade wind blowing
from the shore. Capkin steps out on deck, stretches,
then we both hear a suspicious swish of water off the
starboard side. We move to investigate, and there is
a dolphin staring back up at us. He chirps a greeting,
then continues his investigation of our Zodiac floating
in the water. Setting down my cup of hot chocolate,
Capkin and I slip slowly into the water.

The dolphin immediately swims over to look us
over, and that's when we discover that he has a friend.
Abruptly, there is a group of dolphins swimming and

darting everywhere. To our amazement, they are playing a game with an empty plastic sack. It is a modified
version of tag. A dolphin will snag the plastic sack on
its nose, then try to outswim the other dolphins.
Whoever steals the plastic sack is now "It."

Capkin abruptly gets out of the water, and I wonder where he has gone when he suddenly returns with
the largest pair of flippers I have ever seen. "What are
those?" I ask in surprise.

"Competitive free diver fins," comes the enthusiastic reply. "I'm going to take a turn at capturing that
plastic bag."

Capkin takes a long deep breath, then his long six-
foot, five-inch frame slips beneath the water. The last
part of him to disappear are the long blades of the
giant fins. I hustle out of the water to get a dive mask,
then quickly return to watch the action.

Despite the long fins, Capkin is totally outclassed,
but what he lacks in speed he makes up for in youthful enthusiasm. The dolphins seem to be teasing him,
bringing the plastic sack closer and closer. One dolphin, daring a very close run toward Capkin with the
sack, is abruptly blindsided by another dolphin. The
resulting collision leaves Capkin with the sack firmly
in hand. He rises to the surface, takes a deep breath,
places the sack on his nose, then begins to swim aggressively underwater trying to lure in the dolphins.
Only, they are suddenly tired of the game. One after
another, the group of dolphins heads for the beach,
where the fish truck is just arriving.

Reluctantly, Capkin climbs out of the water with
his hard won plastic sack. He appears to be a little
despondent about not being chased by the dolphins
then remembers he hasn't yet had breakfast. In his
eagerness to get below, he leaves his new pair of
super fins on deck. I wait until the hatch closes, then

quickly put on his monster fins and slip back into the water.

It is amazing how much more quickly I can swim. I dart here and there, and, just about the time I am exhausted, I see a small shape hovering in the water. Bent Fin is back! I swim slowly in her direction, which only causes her to move further away. So, I try staying in one place and click softly. The baby dolphin swims in a little closer but then darts away. Apparently, she prefers people whose feet are firmly planted in the sand. Then, I glance down at the monster fins hanging off my feet. Their long length makes me appear to be over nine feet tall. I must have looked mighty scary to Bent Fin.

For a moment, I'm a little disappointed at not being able to swim with the baby dolphin, but then I realize how lucky I really am. What an awesome opportunity to just be in the water with the two-month-old calf. Floating in the warm ocean, I think how extraordinary it is to be blessed with such an exciting job. I know without doubt that I have never been happier, and I am confident that the rest of my days will also be full of happiness and future adventures. Certainly, things will probably go wrong here and there, but the Lord is my friend and no matter what happens in my life, I will never face adversity, nor carry a burden, alone.

Floating on the surface, watching the dolphins crowd around the few people on the beach begging for fish, I suddenly remember that I haven't eaten yet this morning, either.

A few moments later, the monster fins lay in an abandoned puddle of water on *Alcyone's* deck while I hurry below to see how Capkin is doing with our breakfast.

> *Be bold and courageous. When you look back on your life, you'll regret the things you didn't do more than the ones you did.* (Jackson Brown)

Readers interested in booking Stephen Arrington for motivational and anti-drug presentations at churches or public schools should write:

Stephen Arrington
P.O. Box 3234
Paradise, CA 95967

We welcome any comments from our readers. Feel free to write to us at the following address:

Editorial Department
Huntington House Publishers
P.O. Box 53788
Lafayette, LA 70505

More Good Books from Huntington House

Journey into Darkness: Nowhere to Land
by Stephen L. Arrington

This story begins on Hawaii's glistening sands and ends in the mysterious deep with the Great White Shark. In between, he found himself trapped in the drug smuggling trade—unwittingly becoming the "Fall Guy" in the highly publicized John Z. DeLorean drug case. Naval career shattered, his youthful innocence tested, and friends and family put to the test of loyalty, Arrington locked on one truth during his savage stay in prison and endeavors to share that critical truth now. Focusing on a single important message to young people—to stay away from drugs— the author recounts his horrifying prison experience and allows the reader to take a peek at the source of hope and courage that helped him survive.

ISBN 1-56384-003-3 $9.99

A Jewish Conservative Looks at Pagan America
by Don Feder

With eloquence and insight that rival essayists of antiquity, Don Feder's pen finds his targets in the enemies of God, family, and American tradition and morality. Deftly . . . delightfully . . . the master allegorist and Titian with a typewriter brings clarity to the most complex sociological issues and invokes giggles and wry smiles from both followers and foes. Feder is Jewish to the core, and he finds in his Judaism no inconsistency with an American Judeo-Christian ethic. Questions of morality plague school administrators, district court judges, senators, congressmen, parents, and employers; they are wrestling for answers in a "changing world." Feder challenges this generation and directs inquirers to the original books of wisdom: the Torah and the Bible.

ISBN 1-56384-036-7 Trade Paper $9.99
ISBN 1-56384-037-5 Hardcover $19.99

The Media Hates Conservatives: How It Controls the Flow of Information
by Dale A. Berryhill

Here is clear and powerful evidence that the liberal leaning news media brazenly attempted to influence the outcome of the election between President George Bush and Candidate Bill Clinton. Through a careful analysis of television and newspaper coverage, this book confirms a consistent pattern of liberal bias (even to the point of assisting the Clinton campaign). The major media outlets have taken sides in the culture war. Through bias, distortion, and the violation of professional standards, they have opposed the traditional values embraced by conservatives and most Americans, to the detriment of our country.

ISBN 1-56384-060-X $9.99

ORDER THESE HUNTINGTON HOUSE BOOKS!

- America Betrayed—Marlin Maddoux...................................7.99
- The Assault—Dale A. Berryhill.....................................9.99
- Beyond Political Correctness—David Thibodaux......................9.99
- The Best of HUMAN EVENTS—Edited by James C. Roberts..............34.95
- Can Families Survive in Pagan America?—Samuel Dresner......15.99/31.99 HB
- Circle of Death—Richmond Odom.....................................9.99
- Combat Ready—Lynn Stanley...9.99
- Conservative, American & Jewish—Jacob Neusner.....................9.99
- The Dark Side of Freemasonry—Ed Decker............................9.99
- The Demonic Roots of Globalism—Gary Kah...........................9.99
- Don't Touch That Dial—Barbara Hattemer & Robert Showers.....9.99/19.99 HB
- En Route to Global Occupation—Gary Kah............................9.99
- *Exposing the AIDS Scandal—Dr. Paul Cameron..................7.99/2.99
- Freud's War with God—Jack Wright, Jr..............................7.99
- Goddess Earth—Samantha Smith......................................9.99
- Gays & Guns—John Eidsmoe.....................................7.99/14.99 HB
- Health Begins in Him—Terry Dorian.................................9.99
- Heresy Hunters—Jim Spencer..8.99
- Hidden Dangers of the Rainbow—Constance Cumbey....................9.99
- High-Voltage Christianity—Michael Brown...........................9.99
- Homeless in America—Jeremy Reynolds...............................9.99
- How to Homeschool (Yes, You!)—Julia Toto..........................4.99
- Hungry for God—Larry E. Myers.....................................9.99
- I Shot an Elephant in My Pajamas—Morrie Ryskind w/ John Roberts..12.99
- *Inside the New Age Nightmare—Randall Baer...................9.99/2.99
- A Jewish Conservative Looks at Pagan America—Don Feder.....9.99/19.99 HB
- Journey into Darkness—Stephen Arrington...........................9.99
- Kinsey, Sex and Fraud—Dr. Judith A. Reisman & Edward Eichel.....11.99
- The Liberal Contradiction—Dale A. Berryhill.......................9.99
- Legalized Gambling—John Eidsmoe...................................7.99
- Loyal Opposition—John Eidsmoe.....................................8.99
- The Media Hates Conservatives—Dale A. Berryhill.........9.99/19.99 HB
- New Gods for a New Age—Richmond Odom..............................9.99
- One Man, One Woman, One Lifetime—Rabbi Reuven Bulka..............7.99
- Out of Control—Brenda Scott.............................9.99/19.99 HB
- Outcome-Based Education—Peg Luksik & Pamela Hoffecker.............9.99
- The Parched Soul of America—Leslie Kay Hedger w/ Dave Reagan....10.99
- Please Tell Me—Tom McKenney.......................................9.99
- Political Correctness—David Thibodaux.............................9.99
- Resurrecting the Third Reich—Richard Terrell......................9.99
- Revival: Its Principles and Personalities—Winkie Pratney........10.99
- Trojan Horse—Brenda Scott & Samantha Smith........................9.99
- The Walking Wounded—Jeremy Reynolds...............................9.99

Available in Salt Series

Available at bookstores everywhere or order direct from:
Huntington House Publishers • P.O. Box 53788 • Lafayette, LA 70505
Send check/money order. For faster service use VISA/MASTERCARD.
Call toll-free 1-800-749-4009.
Add: Freight and handling, $3.50 for the first book ordered, and $.50 for
each additional book up to 5 books.